THE

OF ORGANIZING

The Boston Museum of Fine Arts Union Drive

by Michael Raysson

Power Tools for Union Building from Hardball Press

The Union Member's Complete Guide explains in clear language how to get the most out of your job in a unionized workplace, from understanding how a union operates to what you can do to make your union more successful. Topics include the full story on union dues, a union's responsibility to its members, getting help with workplace problems, a member's rights and responsibilities, labor laws that affect you, and much more.

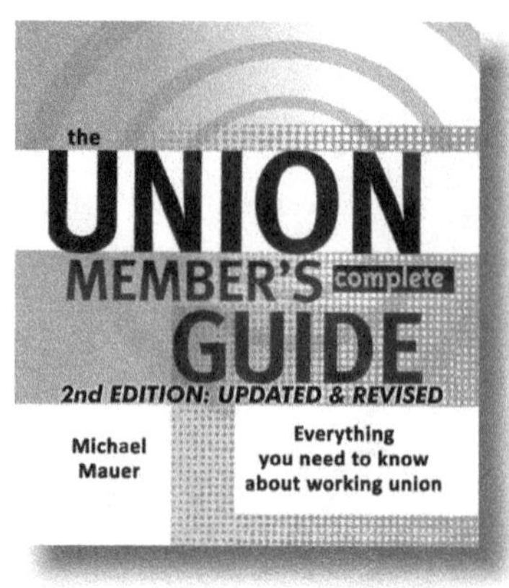

I Just Got Elected, Now What, A New Union Officer's Handbook is a plain-spoken guide that helps leaders evaluate their goals and revitalize their union. Just Elected shows the reader how to mobilize members and breathe fresh vitality into the union. The labor movement isn't about servicing workers, it's about building a sustainable workers' organization, and this handbook shows you how to do it

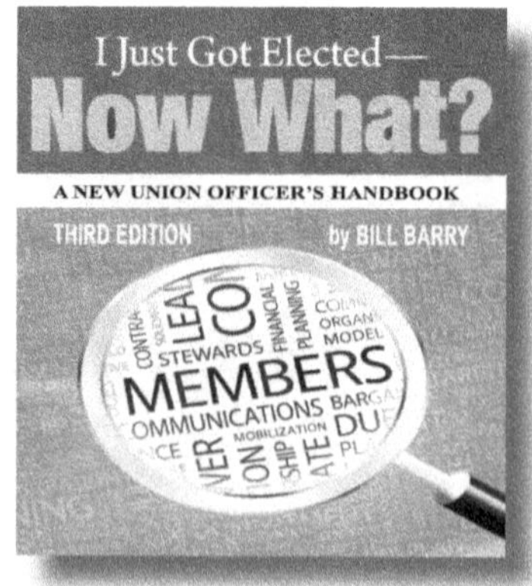

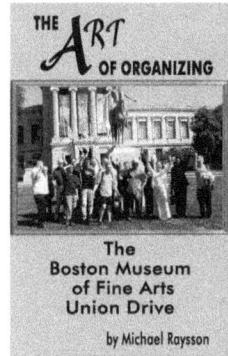

The Art Of Organizing, The Boston Museum of Fine Arts Union Drive,
Published by Hard Ball Press
Book design by D. Bass
ISBN: 978-1-7344938-2-5
Library of Congress Number: 9781734493825
1. Union organizing 2. Labor union 3. Boston Museum of Fine Arts 4. Michael Raysson

DEDICATION

This book is lovingly dedicated to my beloved, beautiful wife, Muriel, whose amazing intelligence has touched all aspects of this book and who has helped me at every step of the way.

ABOUT THE PHOTOS

The photographs in this book were taken more than thirty years ago with a first generation digital camera. The density of the image was low back then. As a result, the images are not as sharp and crisp as they would be with a modern digital camera. Consider them artifacts from an earlier age and enjoy them as you would the art work in the Boston Museum. ~Michael Raysson

Contents

1

I am the people—the mob—the crowd—the mass.
Do you know all the great work of the world is done through me?
I am the working man, the inventor, the maker of the world's food and clothes.
I am the audience that witnesses history.
~*I am the People, the Mob,* Carl Sandburg

BECOMING A PARTICIPANT

The place was the Boston Museum of Fine Arts. In 1988 I was a security guard there. For about six months I thought I was in Paradise.

In the galleries I was amazed. My favorites were the old Chinese painters, and the Museum had a great collection. I loved Chen Rong and his "Nine Dragon Scroll." Old Chen himself said, "At a distance, one feels as if the clouds and waves were flying and moving. Viewed closely, one suspects that only god could have painted these dragons."

I also loved the rooms of the oldest Greeks and their neighbors, the archaic ones. There was no air conditioning in that part of the Museum. It was always hot in there. Very hot. And at that time in my life I loved heat. So I could almost always trade into those galleries with someone who wanted a cooler place, and most guards did. This was especially good for me if I got stuck guarding the "chatchkes."

You could lose yourself in the Colonial basement. And there was one gallery, the "Forsythe Wyckes", which we called "forty winks", because it was so easy to fall asleep in there.

If there was one group of employees who lived up to what you might expect of a world-class Museum, it was the guards. They were of all colors, ethnic groups and nationalities, and many of them were experts in art history. The rest of the Museum staff—with the exception of the cleaners and the utility workers—was lily white. There was a huge segment of guards made up of serious artists, writers, poets, musicians and composers. Then there were guards who had retired from other professions, such as geologists, steel workers, school counselors, chess champions, teachers, Mafia runners, reformed bank robbers and Sears and Roebuck salesmen. Others worked on the side as computer consultants and techies, cosmetic sellers, hairdressers, fast food cart owners. There were waitresses, film makers, actors and actresses, Museum guides, nightclub entertainers, recording artists and you name it. One guard just took classes in his spare time for no good reason except gaining knowledge. His name was Joe Johnson. I remember asking him in the locker room, "Joe, what is your goal in taking all these classes?" *"I don't have any goal. I just want to learn things,"* was his answer. Unfortunately, I never learned what the classes were on.

They came from all political spectrums, from anarchists and socialists to conservatives and Tea Partiers. Many got by on a week-to-week basis. A large segment of those who didn't have side jobs depended on overtime.

Ed Gonski, who got me the job at the Museum, was always lecturing one or another of the patrons in his galleries on the art there. His favorite, though, was the Minoan Snake Goddess, whose authenticity later became the subject of great controversy. Jim Beneway, a supervisor, said that if no one was around, Ed would lecture the wall. Jim himself was someone many guards lived in fear of. They called him "Rambo".

Radcliffe Small, who was next to me in the locker room was one of a small contingent from the island of Barbados. He was learning from Dave Hebden how to pick up the Japanese girls who often came to the Museum. Jean (I forget his last name), from Haiti, didn't need any lessons. Chin Wah was the elder statesman, but he didn't say much. Well, Nickolai, from Russia, might have been even older. He would point at the children who passed by and say, "Dangerous creatures!"

Lisa Rhea was small, but feisty as all get out. She was also one the the smartest people in the Museum, but a classic underachiever. Lisa and her half-sister Brenda were long-time African American residents of Cambridge, a community next door to the Museum. Her mother was a schoolteacher. But there was a lot of history in that family that was hard to figure out.

Jill Abatemarco was a beautiful artist who had graduated from MassArt, just down the road. (Her brother, Michael, an actor, was also a guard.) Dave Hebden was once a famous surfer down in South Carolina. Along with Lisa and myself, this would be the foursome that later negotiated our first Union contract.

Most of the work we did as guards was fairly cut and dry. But getting to know the intricacies of the overtime details was pretty daunting. Standing in line one morning every week at 6:00 a.m., there would always be a great number of guards waiting to sign up. I asked Brenda, who was already an old-timer, for some help in understanding what was going on. "You'll catch on, Raysson," said Brenda, "It just takes time." When I entered the room, I saw a bunch of papers tacked on the walls all around the room, each with a different overtime option. People scurried about, some signing everything in sight.

At first, when things began to change, I could not have told you what was happening, only that working conditions were getting worse for security guards: from not being able to go to the bathroom and not being able to sit down, to losing long-time benefits. We had a new boss, a former State Police Sergeant, Bill McAuliffe, and he was mean. He didn't like art, he didn't like guards and he didn't like who we were. We didn't like him either. It was hostility, verging on out and out war at first sight.

Although we didn't know it, we were witnessing the emergence of the corporate takeover of cultural institutions in America and around the world. Probably no one on the Museum staff or in the Museum World understood what was really happening. That understanding came a few years later, horribly and suddenly, after a Brit named Malcolm Rogers was hired to direct the Museum. He instituted what was called "The Boston Massacre." But more on that later.

It is difficult to put the union experience in proper perspective without first giving a clear picture of how the takeover took place and what was there before.

The Pre-Corporate Museum for the Guards

The Boston Museum of Fine Arts is a private institution. In a way, it is (or was) a private club of the Boston Brahmins, opened up by their largesse to the public. At one time, it was free to anyone and everyone. There is still a sign, now covered over, which proudly proclaims this fact. One part of this tradition, which was still very much in evidence when I began working there, was the idea of a "Museum Family." Certainly there was a large amount of *noblesse oblige* in this picture. Still, it was legitimate and sincere. At bottom, it was based on a mutual appreciation of the art, whether you were curating it, protecting it or cleaning its environs. This feeling spread all the way up the ladder to the members of the Board. They loved to rub elbows with curators who were top experts in their field. They loved to be received at the door by guards who greeted them by name.

The pre-corporate Museum was not ideal, but in an archaic way it seemed so. The fact that we were paid a mere pittance didn't seem to matter that much. While the pay was abysmally low, the benefits seemed magnificent. There were 24 (yes, 24!) sick days to be had. We could save holidays and then take them whenever we chose (and, amazingly, no one in management hassled us about it). The shifts were staggered so that every other week we had a three-day weekend. We had the same excellent health and retirement plans as management. For every one dollar we put in the retirement plan, three dollars would be added.

The biggest perk, of course, was that we got to hang out in the galleries and look at the art. If we had to go to the bathroom, or just wanted to take a short break, we only had to ask the guard next to us to keep an eye on our galleries. The same for lunch. Neighboring guards took over while we ate our lunch, and then we did the same for them. It was no big deal if someone came back a little late.

There were chairs in the gallery. If we needed to sit, we could sit, as long as we were reasonable about it. After all, standing up all day is not easy, especially for older guards. The number of guards with back, feet and other related problems was extremely large.

The head of security at that time was a retired FBI agent, Tom Manning. He was tall and gaunt. Actually, we rarely saw him. Mainly he stayed in his office, where he had a nice desk to put his feet up, and a good salary. Other than that, he didn't do much. And that was fine. His attitude toward us guards was, "live and let live."

Six months after entering this idyllic atmosphere, everything changed. It was not a gradual change but a sudden one, and in many ways, disastrous from the point of view of a security guard. You might call it "Paradise Lost." The "it" came in the form of a new director of security with a whole new philosophy of running the place. In its harshness and severity, it made the word "Draconian" come to mind.

2

You manufactured conflict
long hours and little pay
...But together we can beat you
together we all hold sway

~*Capitalism's Progress,* John Tomlinson

TESTING THE WATERS

More often than not it is management, not the workers that makes a labor union.

After I had worked half a year at the Museum, the old director of security, Tom Manning, retired. I don't know whether it was forced or voluntary, but the new director, Bill McAuliffe, a former state police sergeant, came on with a vengeance.

In short, the happy days of the security guards turned sour. The changes were both petty and serious. Special guards were hired to cover our lunch breaks. The special guards had no scheduled lunch break, but of course, they expected one. This only happened if everyone returned exactly on time. Lunch, which used to be an easy going and happy time of day for us, became the scene of intense fights. There was a not so gradual loss of those marvellous benefits and perks I have mentioned. Sick days were cut in half.

In the past it was understood that guards worked on a staggered schedule which changed from week to week. As a result, that there would always be some full-time guards who would miss out on certain holidays because of the demands of their particular schedule. Nevertheless, they were given credit and they could still get the extra holiday pay or choose a day off of their choice. Suddenly, they neither got the extra holiday pay or a day off.

With the new rules, many guards lost all chance of getting holiday time off. The overtime schedule was changed and those who worked it came under heavy scrutiny.

Guards could no longer break for each other. If you had to go to the bathroom, you had to wait for a supervisor. Sometimes this could be hours. When the supervisor came, you had to go to the nearest bathroom. If the supervisor thought you took too long or that you hadn't gone to the nearest bathroom, you could be disciplined. I listened to outrageous stories told to me by guards who were harassed for supposedly taking too long to do their business or were given the third degree as to which bathroom they had used. "Raysson, what are we going to do?' said Tina. "I can't even go to the bathroom of my choice! And then they tell me how long it has to take! I'm not a little kid. I can't work like that!"

Guards could only sit in certain galleries. In others, they had to stand all day. If a guard was caught sitting, even for a short while, they could be severely disciplined. Standing all day, day after day, was dangerous and debilitating to a guard's health, causing chronic medical conditions that lasted for the rest of their lives. Maureen Roe came to me. "Can they just take away our chairs like that and make us stand all day? Can't we do anything to stop them?"

All in all, it was demeaning. It caused squabbles and worse. Most of the changes were just plain unfair.

The fact that we made chicken feed suddenly became a lot more important to us. And just like that, the idea of a labor union was seemingly born out of nothing, like the Big Bang.

3

You got to talk to the workers in the shop with you
You got to build you a union...

~*Talking Union* by Lee Hays,
Millard Lampell and Pete Seeger

THE BEGINNING

Management not only makes labor unions but, in my case, union organizers. In retrospect, they took away my ideal and my idyll and replaced them with something more valuable, that I had no idea existed in me—working with and for others.

The 1980s were ending. The 1990s were beginning. Looking back, what reason was there for Museum management to hassle its guards? Certainly we weren't costing them a lot of money. We weren't any trouble. No one was complaining. The curators liked us. The patrons liked us. Even the trustees liked us.

Ah, but there's the rub. Let me change that to "the old-time trustees liked us." Now there was an entirely new type of trustee. They were not Brahmins, they were businessmen. There may even have been a woman or two. They were CEOs and lawyers of large corporations.

The new trustees saw the Museum in a different light. It was not about art appreciation. It was not about a "Museum Family." It was not about sharing your art with the public. It was about business.

So they took away benefits. They took away our freedom. And they took away our chairs. Our *chairs*! That was the straw that broke the camel's back—and hurt many of ours. But what did they know about the backs and legs and feet of security guards?

My friend Dave Hebden and I would commiserate with each other about all this, and try to figure out what the guards should do as we rode our bikes home together at night. We would have long discussions until we reached home.

In 1991, word began to go around in guard circles. That word was "*Union.*" Pretty soon almost every guard was saying it. I remember a small group of guards, committed to unionizing, would get together after work, meeting in a secret cabal, looking to find out what we could do. The search was on—how to organize a union?

4

I have a pact with love and beauty
I have a pact of blood with my people...
--from *Do Not Ask Me* by Pablo Neruda

LEADING UP TO...

Often, seemingly chance happenings change lives. So it was with me. In 1991, I had two weeks off for what was going to be a very important vacation for me. At the very last moment, though, plans for my trip were cancelled and there was nothing I could do.

I had a free two weeks. What to do with them? I have said that the *idea* of a labor union was going around in Museum guard circles at that time. But no one really knew anything about organizing a union, least of all me.

I had never had the slightest inclination in that direction. I had never been any kind of leader. I had never shown any proclivity towards social activism. Until then.

I decided to spend those two weeks researching labor unions. I learned a lot and began to relate it to our conditions at the Museum of Fine Arts. I found out about organizing a union in general, but I also found that our position at the Museum was unique. We were security guards working at a private institution. Therefore, we were under the restrictions of the Taft- Hartley Act, which made us different from almost everyone else.

As private security guards, we were forbidden to join AFL-CIO unions unless we had management's permission (more about this law later on). I knew that was hardly likely to happen. More research told me, however, that there existed an "international" security guard union, especially for people like us.

I found out how to get in touch with them, and did. In short, when I returned two weeks later, I was—if only by comparison to everyone else at the Museum—an expert. I communicated my newfound knowledge to others. We needed to get as many people as possible to sign union cards, which was the way to start election proceedings—by taking the signed cards to the Labor Board. We needed to decide when was the proper time to do that. Of course, I needed to explain what the Labor Board was, and how management would come after us like anything once they found out what we were up to. We began to meet at the houses and apartments of various guards, including my own. I was the one they looked to for advice. It just kind of happened.

I don't really remember all of the people who attended those early secret meetings. The one who I most remember was Pearl, the woman who manned the uniform room. She took in dirty uniforms and handed out clean ones. She knew everyone and talked to everyone. She probably was the most influential member of the guard force. She was from the Caribbean islands, had a deep accent and talked in the idiom of that area. In the beginning she was one of our biggest pro-union activists and the best person to have on your side. But in the middle of the campaign, something changed. While many people came and went in and out of the union over the years, no one did it so completely and so suddenly as Pearl. I didn't dare even approach her about it. No one did. So it was left to rumor and supposition. I can only say that she operated a little ice cream wagon right in front of the Museum to make some extra money. It was thought that this was against Museum rules. Many people who I talked to thought she got that privilege in return for staying away from the union. To this day I wonder about it.

Michael Power, a young guard who often hung out with Pearl, was a regular at these meetings, as were Jeff Rowecamp and Russell Gilfoy, a faithful union man until he retired from the Museum. Jeff Erickson and Dean Stevens came in from the night crew.

Finally, Jill Abatemarco, Dave Hebden and Lisa Rhea, who were all to be on our negotiating team, were there most of the time.

Except for Russell Gilfoy who had helped to form a Teachers' Union, we were all in unknown waters here. "What can they do to us?" "Can we get fired?" "Is it worth it?" You can imagine there was a lot of discussion on these subjects. Jill Abatemarco talked about how much she had liked the Museum at first, but now it had turned into an oppressive, unfriendly place and that we had to change that. Here, we all agreed with her. We weren't sure of the first two questions and we were definitely scared about them, but we still decided whether or not they could or would try to fire us it was worth it. I remember that Russell tried to reassure us by saying that no one at his school lost their jobs.

Besides the logistics of joining a union and having an election that we could win, much of our discussions centered around creating a communication system, so that we had regular contact with the other guards and could get a pulse on our overall direction. We began to subtly question everyone to find out where they stood. We began to plan our strategy to get the Union Cards signed and hand them in to the National Labor Relations Board.

There were also many questions about the national security guard union. When my co-workers wanted to find out more about it or communicate with it, I was the go-to guy. It was called the United Plant Guard Workers of America, or UPGWA. I brought their plans and communiqués to our secret meetings. Gradually, we built up a strategy and a plan, and we found out the steps leading up to unionizing: spreading the word—quietly convincing others, signing union cards, holding an election.

UPGWA sent us packets designed to disseminate information on how to deal with the various situations one might encounter in organizing. The packets were quite helpful. At this point, they were right on the money in their assistance.

The people who were there at the meetings in the beginning were not necessarily the ones who were in the forefront when we actually held the election. And these people changed again when we won the election and had to negotiate a contract. Over the years, this dynamic of change would continue. Only a very few people remained deeply committed from the beginning to the end, when I left 17 years later. I was one of them. But the others were heroes of the Museum guards, well worth remembering.

At any rate, this was the way it happened in the beginning, when things came together and I realized the unfairness of the situation we were in. When I saw that management had become bullies, and the more they bullied, the more they liked it. I realized not only that I didn't like that, but that I could do something about it—or should I say, "*we* could do something about it." I also realized how much I liked the idea. More so, I realized that I could really help others by the process of banding together and I liked that too. Mostly, however, I learned that gathering people to work together for empowerment and common cause against a powerful tyrant was not foreign to my being. It was intrinsic.

This is how I became a leader.

5

They'll swear that they're your friend, won't they lie?
They'll swear to make amends, won't they lie?
--from Didn't They Lie *by Jack Warshaw*

THE BATTLE IS JOINED

It now came down to putting the logistics we learned into practice and working through the limitations enforced by the Taft-Hartley Act. The Taft-Hartley Act was also known as the Labor Relations Act of 1947, but labor leaders called it the "Slave Labor Bill." In it, security guards in the private sector are not allowed to join an AFL or CIO union—they were separate at the time—unless given permission to do so by management. Mighty unlikely. At the time, this part of the bill was OK with Labor because of the bad blood with Pinkerton security guards who had worked for management to end union strikes—often in a very bloody manner. We wanted to wait until the right time to have our fellow guards sign union cards to hold an official vote for a union. The "right time" is pretty much when you feel you have maximized the number of workers who are behind the idea of a union and are ready to act on it, while keeping it secret from management.

We knew it took just over 50% of the vote to win, but we also knew that you should have a 75–80% favourable vote in the beginning because management would winnow the number down.

When the cards were handed in and the cat was out of the bag, the campaign began in earnest. Anti-union campaigns are pretty much all orchestrated in the same manner. In that way UPGWA was ahead of the game.

They told us what management would say and management said it.

UPGWA Advisory Letter

DEAR BROTHERS AND SISTERS

Now is the time for solidarity. Be aware that the administration has started their campaign and will use many subtle methods to intimidate or persuade us.

When the higher-ups come around asking about problems or complaints, aside from tossing us a few bones, the main purpose is merely to find "ringleaders" or "troublemakers" whom they can pinpoint; likewise in morning talks.

Similarly, supervisors and others may hint such things as we will lose all benefits and start again from zero, or that we could lose our jobs, etc. Such things are blatantly untrue (we are protected on these and many other counts by law). So do not be frightened, bullied, or tempted.

We all know that up till now our discontent was treated with "If you don't like it--there's the door!" Strange these people are suddenly so caring.

So remember our strength lies in keeping together and not giving in. By helping one another we help ourselves.

Above, an advisory letter from UPGWA, one of many they sent, schooling us in the ways that management handles these campaigns.

In addition to this letter, Dave Hebden had a good friend who was a union organizer from local 26, the hotel workers' union. We got a lot of good information from him. "Here's what's going to happen," he told Dave, "They're going to hire some union busting consultants and lawyers, and those people will come in frequently to meet with supervisors and the director of security. They are going to give them all sorts of threatening information to tell the guards, such as: "You'll probably lose your health benefits" and "Dues will cost you $75-$100 a month," and so on. The supervisors will disseminate this "information" to all the guards. Management will have the full roster, and they'll make a scorecard of those who seem like they will vote "yes" for the union and those who seem like they'll vote "no" and those who are on the fence." "After they find out where guards stand, they will target those who look like they are going to vote "yes" and those who are on the fence. And they will frighten them with all sorts of disinformation."

So, we countered that with our own system. We formed a network of guards who would find out what the supervisors were saying. Whenever the supervisors came around, these people would question various of our people to ascertain what methods the supervisors were currently using to scare the guards. They would see which guards were indeed scared, which ones were tending toward voting against the union, which ones were on the fence and which ones were strong and would vote "yes."

We already knew a lot of what management would tell the guards even before they said it.

Gail Mallard, the dark queen of Human Resources, who up till then was known for giving guards a hard time, suddenly put on a happy, smiling face. "The Museum loves and respects you. If you have any problems please come into my office and I will be happy to work it out with you. Let us work together and keep away from this adversarial business!" Supervisor Ralph was simple and to the point. "Don't get involved in this bullshit. It won't help you. It'll just make things worse." Supervisor Robert: "It just isn't sensible for you to join a union. You'll lose money paying dues. You'll make enemies. You don't need this aggravation. Neither do we. Do you understand all the problems you would bring upon yourselves?"

We passed around sheets beforehand showing why the guards shouldn't believe them. Management will almost always tell unionizing workers (as they told the guards in our case) that when a union is voted in, workers lose money by paying union dues. We would show that, in point of fact, statistics show that the amount of money the average union worker makes, as compared to what a non-union worker makes doing the same job, far outweighs the amount a member pays out for dues, not to speak of the many other advantages union representation gives to the worker, such as increased overtime, health and sickness benefits and protections, to name just a few.

Management will also almost always say that unions bring on a confrontational relationship with management. In our case, management had already proved themselves to be antagonistic to our concerns. Their treatment of us belied their words. In fact, it made them look bald facedly hypocritical. So that was easy to counter. In this way, we would show, in advance of management even putting forth the argument, how such assertions were not really true.

By the time the supervisors made their points, we had already told the guards why they were wrong. The guards had heard it all and knew the truth about it.

When we learned about those points which the supervisors were disseminating that hadn't already been countered, we had our fast response network, which would then answer these points in just a few hours. Of course, we were very low tech at the time. For the most part, we communicated by handwritten mimeographed leaflets. Fortunately, I have pretty good handwriting. Still, it is a little embarrassing to look back at our work then, even though it worked well enough.

The guards in our networks would also work to shore up those guards who were on the fence or were scared of what they were told, in spite of our counter information. This is how two of them talked about it:

KC: Well...I'm tired of all this. I don't really care, anyway.
Network Guard: KC, It's time you stood up for something.
KC: But I don't really care.
Network Guard: That's not what you told me before, when you were complaining about all the things management is doing.
KC: Well...I don't know, Larry.
NETWORK GUARD: Like when you missed having a lunch break...
KC: Well...
NETWORK GUARD: Like Beneway the supervisor harassing you every day...
KC: (long pause)
NETWORK GUARD: Like being disciplined for being late when public transportation had broken down...
KC: (long pause)
NETWORK GUARD: These are things that having a union can change for you.
KC: But what about all the dues I'll have to pay?
NETWORK GUARD: Remember that raise you never get and always complain about? A union will get you that raise which will more than compensate for any little bit of dues you have to pay.
KC: (long pause again) Wow. I can't believe it. Those are some pretty good points. I really have to rethink this. I hate to admit it but the union just might be the way to go, Larry.

Certain people who were very pro-union were nevertheless stressed out by the constant pressure put on them by supervisors. We heard from a guard who told us about his girlfriend who was feeling like this. She was very shy. One of the main reasons she had taken a job at the Museum was because it had an atmosphere where she could get away from stress. When we investigated, we found there were many others like this.

So we advised the guards who were communicating with them to tell these people to just let their supervisors think they were going to vote "no", and then the supervisors would probably leave them alone. That worked.

Another part of our plan was a spy network consisting of the parking lot guards. Whenever the consultants or lawyers arrived at the Museum, they immediately put the word out.

In this way we were able to keep ahead of management. It wasn't easy, because the guards had so many different shifts. But somehow we managed and managed well.

There are other ways in which management does have a huge advantage when their workers are trying to form unions. One which they used on us in large measure was calling forced assemblies to put across their points. We all had to attend and listen whether we liked it or not. They were sure to make all the canned points the union-busting consultants told them to make. For example, in the assemblies, management claimed that Union dues would take a huge portion of our salary, that people in Unions do worse than non-Union people, that unions just tell a bunch of lies to their members, and so on, all offered as unassailable facts. I suppose they thought that if even the Director of the Museum stated such things, we would automatically accept them as true.

The Museum Director and the Assistant Director would often be present at these assemblies to put in their two cents.

Management will invest hundreds of thousands of dollars in employing companies that specialize in busting or preventing unions. Quite often, much more money will be spent on these companies than the added expenses of dealing with unions and paying higher wages, etc. I am convinced that corporations have more fear of giving a voice and power to workers, and thereby losing some of their control, than giving workers higher wages and better benefits.

Another method management used was full court pressure. When the end was close upon us, the supervisors, members of Human Resources and the director of security all conspired to try to intimidate any guard they thought they could turn to their side. Interspersed in these conversations or monologues from management officials would be tidbits from the Union Busters playbook, not the least being implied threats of losing our jobs and getting disciplined while gaining nothing and losing everything in the process, and above all that we were weak and powerless against management.

The tension was immense.

6

What's that I see a coming?
It's that Union Train a coming...
--from *Union Train* by the Almanac Singers

THE WORKER'S VOICE

Voting day, May 16, 1991: One after another the members stepped into the booth and cast their ballots.

Management was sure that their pressure had worked and that it was just a little time before things returned to normal. Like the good sports they were, they would shake hands with us, perhaps get rid of the trouble-makers if they could, and be done with it. That is what the union busters and lawyers had prophesized. Surely, management's hard work would not go unrewarded.

On our side, we hoped our fellow guards would vote the way they promised us. We knew that once they were inside the booth, alone with management's threats in their ears and hearts, they could cave in and vote "no" and no one would know the difference.

We were scared.

Finally, with the Labor Board observer, ourselves and management watching, the votes began to be counted. One after another, the votes were "yes" and again "yes'! It was even greater than we hoped—a landslide for the union, 80-18.

[Please see page 26 for the UPGWA's response to our victory:]

Management sent out a note as well.

[Please see page 27 for the Museum Director's response.]

Suddenly we had a union. We had not gotten fired. Now we had protection and we had a platform.

The UPGWA's response to our victory

CONGRATULATIONS and
Welcome
whether you were "FOR"
or "AGAINST"
NOW IT'S
"TEAMWORK TIME"

Now we have a union. We have it because more of us wanted it than didn't want it. Now it's time to make our union good . . . make it an instrument of progress for all . . . and that takes all of us working together.

Starting right now the "PAST" is PASSED. Whether you fought for or against makes no difference now. We're all in the same family and TEAMWORK is the key to PROGRESS.

There's nothing more American than a good battle at election time. But it's also very "American" to all join together for progress after the majority has spoken.

There were lots of good people on both sides of this campaign. We need all of them on the same side of the campaign that now faces us. The most critical period for building good unions is now. If all of us make up our minds that the union is going to be Good, then it will be good!

Now that we've established our union, the time is here to develop it. That means setting up committees, drafting by-laws, compiling our proposals and preparing for our negotiations with the company.

There's a spot in the union program for every one of us who wants to be part of this great effort to improve ourselves. The hand of the union and everyone who fought for it is extended in friendship to all. Let's make it a real TEAMWORK operation.

THE "VICTORY VOTE"

UPGWA

80

NO UNION

18

While the official tally of the vote has been made by the NLRB, it takes a few days for the actual certification to come through. In the meantime we'll be developing our union. Watch for any announcements and be sure to take part in any and all meetings as they are called. Remember, there's a great deal to be done and a place for everyone.

CONTACT:

UPGWA

ORGANIZING DEPARTMENT

UNITED PLANT GUARD WORKERS OF AMERICA

The Museum Director's response

TO: All Staff

FROM: Alan Shestack
Mort Golden

DATE: May 17, 1991

As you may know already, the International Union, United Plant Guard Workers of America, received a majority of the votes cast in yesterday's election.

We must caution you that the results are unofficial. The Museum and the union have seven days to file any objections to the election with the NLRB. The union cannot be certified as the representative of the guards until after this seven-day period expires. During this period, we must follow the same guidelines that were in effect during the campaign.

Needless to say, we are disappointed with this outcome, but we, nevertheless, respect the guards' right to make this choice.

Some of you may feel that if the Protective Services Department has a union representing them that you need one as well. We hope that the majority of you agree that this is not the case. Further, we want to assure you that the results of this election will have no impact upon our relationship with non-security staff. We want you to know that we will continue to do all we can to be responsive to our entire staff and continue to deal with you in a responsible and professional manner.

As always, if you have any questions, concerns, or problems, you should feel free to discuss them with your supervisor or the Human Resources Department. In addition, if you have any particular questions about the election or the impact that the guards' union will have on you or your department, your supervisor or Human Resources will be more than happy to discuss the situation further.

MJG:AS/nbe

RESULT
FOR UNION 80
AGAINST " 18

We could pinch ourselves! All the work and strategizing we had done so far had *really* worked. But we had yet to learn a myriad of lessons, some easy, many difficult in the extreme. Our next step into the unknown would be negotiating our first contract.

7

But believe it or not
You won't find it so hot
If you ain't got the do re mi
~from *Do Re Mi* by Woodie Guthrie

THE CONTRACT

The first thing that happens after a union victory is the beginning of contract negotiations with management. Following the successful vote, the contract campaign was on. But really, we didn't know much about conducting an outside contract campaign—and UPGWA didn't teach us much. We were totally ignorant about reaching out to the media or other groups. Most of that we learned only later.

Our negotiating team consisted of Jill Abatemarco, Dave Hebden, Lisa Rhea and myself. Jill was a young artist not too long out of Massachusetts College of Art, just down the street from the Museum. I remember her at that time as a breath of fresh air—young, sweet, and smart. Dave and Lisa were savvy, wise in the ways of the world and quick learners in this all-too-new process. John Baumler, the negotiator from UPGWA, was our front man. He was crusty, knowledgeable and a bit cynical. In retrospect, very cynical. UPGWA had dredged him up out of a very comfortable retirement in Florida. Perhaps he needed some extra cash.

Given what I know now about negotiations, working with UPGWA was bizarre. They taught us nothing about contract issues. We were left entirely on our own. They did give us a list of possible negotiation points. There were lots and lots of things on it. We went over it like a mail order catalogue. Certainly, the guards had a lot of needs.

For four hectic weeks, we met together and we came up with a huge contract offer sheet listing demands relating to practically every issue that we could think of or conjure up. We put in everything from gallery coverage to wages and hundreds of things in between. We had no idea *that the chances of our getting 99% of those issues was zilch*. Baumler never let on. Later, Dave deduced that since Baumler was probably being paid by the day, he was happy to draw things out as long as possible. The same went for the Museum lawyer.

The line on negotiating as a union is that you pick your top two or three issues and fight hard as hell for them. Then you have four or five other issues that you would like to win, but are expendable. But Baumler laid out each and every issue we had written up before management, making an argument for each one, knowing full well they were going nowhere. The negotiations went on for many long months. It seemed as if we were hopelessly deadlocked.

Finally, *finally*, a mediator was called in from the Federal Mediation Service, and we got down to real business—or "boilerplate" as Baumler called it. Then, and only then, we began to realize what we could really achieve, and things rapidly moved to the endgame.

We had eliminated the "kitchen sink" and almost everything else, time off with pay for childbirth, increased food allowance for overtime over four hours, more sensible gallery coverage, more chairs, a very hefty pay raise and various protections we wanted in, etc. While this was way, way less than what we had started with, it was still more than they were even willing to look at.

The last two days we were up all day, all night and into the wee morning hours. It looked like we were hopelessly deadlocked, but early one morning management put a "final contract" or "last, best and final offer" on the table.

The Museum's offer had double time and a half holiday pay for all full-timers, time and a half for all non-holiday overtime and stuff like that. This was good because overtime was one the most important issues for guards barely getting by. Vacations were two weeks at the beginning going up to five weeks after 20 years. But vacations were not a big deal for most guards. They wanted work.

Forget about gallery coverage and anything like that in the final offer. Health benefits had to be the same as management, there was nothing they could do about that. Sick leave was back to 12 days. This and a few other things fit into Baumler's "boilerplate" business that is in most union contracts. Chairs and bathroom breaks were not going to be in there, but it was unofficially agreed that we would be allowed "brief respite sitting" and that we wouldn't be hassled if we took a "reasonable" time for a bathroom break. Strangely, they pretty much kept to that unofficial part of the agreement. It was the pay raise that was the huge problem for everyone, including management. No one on either side really understood the complicated step process.

But there it was, take it or leave it. All four of us had to unanimously accept the offer. In addition, we had to fully recommend it to our members at a ratification meeting.

The mediator went over all the points and explained it as best he could. There was a complicated stepped-raise pay scale that changed every year. I took copious notes, but still the four of us were confused and dazed. What to do? A decision had to be made. If we didn't accept it, we would for all intents and purposes be back where we were at the beginning, though possibly a little older and a little wiser.

We adjourned to caucus together. I was against accepting it. Dave was for accepting it and letting the members decide. "But we have to tell them that we unanimously recommend it," I countered. Jill and Lisa were somewhere in between. By this time, Dave and Baumler were very much at odds with each other. Dave plain didn't think Baumler was on the up and up. As it later turned out, he was right. Tempers became short between them. "Dave, something must have happened to you in your life, because you don't trust anyone," said Baumler at one point. Dave answered, "Well, something did happen to me. But I have lost faith in this process."

After much debate, we decided to accept the contract. Amazingly, although no one realized it, it was a good contract for the union. We were hugely disappointed, of course, what with all our expectations. I think that the interim negotiating confused everybody, including the management team. UPGWA's philosophy of ultimately achieving the same wage for all their workers regardless of seniority necessitated a very complicated wage scale. The irony of it was that the Museum probably thought they were getting a good deal and we thought we were getting a bad one. It was just the opposite.

The raise for the first year averaged between one and six percent per worker, so it averaged out to about three percent for the first year, and then a step raise for the following two years.

We had reason to be proud and happy, even if we couldn't recognise it.

8

They been and throwed the concept out the door.
--from *A Contract Ain't A Contract Anymore*
by Robert D. Stubbs

BETRAYAL

Actually, it turned out that the raise we got was too good. The Museum realized they had been too generous. But, believing they had found a loophole based on a technicality in the wording, they reneged in the third year on the negotiated raise. If this were to be upheld, we would lose all the step raises we should have gained in the second and third year of the contract.

Of course, we expected UPGWA to come to our aid. I had taken copious notes based on the mediator's explanation of the contract at the very end of our negotiations. These notes clearly showed that there was no problem with the way the wage scale was being handled by management in the previous two years.

So I felt all we had to do was to get the mediator to verify the notes. But then came an unexpected bombshell. UPGWA sided with management! We were staggered. How was it possible?

We have no clear evidence in hand, but years later a night watch guard told me that he had seen what we all suspected. Going through the administrative offices on his rounds, he had found, lying around on someone's desk, a letter of collusion between the Museum and the union. You see, it is part of the night watch guards' job to be sure everything is all right and secure in all areas of the Museum, including the administrative offices on the third floor. I wish we had a copy of that letter, but the guard on the night shift had no way of copying it.

To be honest, we had been having problems with UPGWA right from the beginning. Upon researching this matter of the Museum refusing to give us our raise, I discovered that John Baumler, the UPGWA representative who negotiated the contract with us, had agreed with management's position. When I wrote a letter to the president of the Union, Baumler obfuscated. In the meantime, Kerry Lacey, our local's group leader, upheld Baumler's interpretation in the third step of our grievance on the matter. Obviously, it was no use going to arbitration when our own Union would bear witness against us.

At this time I brought in McCarthy to advocate for us. We didn't think we would win the case (we didn't), but at least we were making a statement and setting a precedent in having McCarthy be our man. Thereby, we introduced him to our members as someone who would fight for our cause.

The union was slow to file grievances, too. Kerry Lacy was a hard guy to find. Grievances which went beyond the first step and needed his attendance as our representative would go on for months and months because he never showed up. Neither would he answer our phone calls or letters until weeks or months after we called or sent them. Then he would act if that was just the natural way to go about such business or, worse, make a joke about it. The worst unions usually have a terrible record backing their members in the grievance process, or, for that matter, having their back in any type of case. Members in these types of unions often come to feel that their officers at the top are little better than management. They are probably right.

David Jones, who at this time was running for UPGWA president in a bid to unseat the powers that be in the union, had this to say: "Ask yourself the last time that you have seen an International Executive at your Local Union Meeting to listen to your views and concerns. I can't remember *even one* at local 109 in 12 years!"

Later, we found out that group leaders and negotiators for UPGWA made around $90,000 a year and the union president made over $100,000. According to Jones, the President made $102,000 a year. Once a year, the union had a convention in some place like Las Vegas, where these guys could use their huge expense accounts. It was a good life for them, but sad for the local unions they supposedly serviced, including us.

The writing was on the wall. The guards were disillusioned and disheartened: "Is this what a union is like?" Many guards did lose hope, but others came to me to ask for help.

At this time, I was working mainly as Head Shop Steward, trying to make our grievance system run in spite of Lacey. Lisa Rhea was the President, and she came to me: "Mikey, we need you to get more involved! Everyone has lost faith in the Union. All that we worked so hard for is falling apart!" So I jumped into the fire. The question was: "What, if anything, can we do?"

Good question. What to do? I found out that there was a window of opportunity when the contract was up in which to disengage from the union by a vote of the membership. It was also possible at the time of this window to vote in another union.

Once again, we made secret plans. Mostly, those who met in secret were the ones who had worked so hard to form the union and make it successful, the ones who did the nitty gritty day-to-day work, who did not want to see all that work go down the drain.

Honestly, I don't know what those guys at UPGWA thought we would do. They had just completely crippled us and demoralized our membership! Their greed for money seemed so great that they appeared to be willing to sell us down the river after only two years. Did they think we would sit still and take it?

I don't believe they cared.

9

We can bring to birth a new world
From the ashes of the old.
--from *Solidarity Forever* by Ralph Chaplin

AN INDEPENDENT UNION

Once in the galleries I ran into my friend Dave Hebden, who had helped to start the union. Dave was intelligent and insightful and had a good sense of humor. He was one of the main persons who had helped to devise the strategy which had been vital to our winning the election of a security guard union at the Museum.

He said to me, "You know, Mike, we missed the boat. If we had played our cards right, we could have worked our way into one of UPGWA's group leader positions. We could have $90,000 a year, plus expenses. And once a year, we could have gone free of charge to one of their great conventions."

Dave Hebden in his guard uniform, 1994, at the MFA

Dave knew our negotiator from the International, John Baumler, quite well, and had already distrusted him even before he and the union betrayed us. Dave had been a skilled woodworker until the fumes from the chemicals he used in his work had done him in. Previous to that, he had been a surfer of some repute in South Carolina, where he was nicknamed, "Duke" after the legendary Duke Paoa Kahanamoku, the godfather of all surfers.

Dave suggested I go check out Jobs With Justice, a new organization at that time which helped labor unions and other social justice causes. Jobs With Justice still exists, with chapters all over the country. It is a progressive organization, which is on the front lines of labor and other social movements. It is probably the foremost group of its type. Locally, it has been headed for many years by Russ Davis.

Rand Wilson was the head. Jobs With Justice was only one stop, albeit an important one, on Rand's lifelong journey of union organizing and social activism. He started as an organizer in the Oil, Chemical and Atomic Workers (OCAW), before coming to JWJ; then there was the Communication Workers Union (CWA), the Teamsters Union, the AFL-CIO and the Service Employees Union (SEIU). In addition, he was national coordinator of "Labor for Bernie" (Sanders).

Rand said, "You could go to the union for security guards at Harvard University, but, as far as I can tell, they are just as bad as the one you already have."

He then suggested that I should go see Phil Mamber, the head of the very progressive UE Electrical Workers Union.

I did. Phil was one of the kindest and most helpful men I have ever met. He looked like a kind of beardless Santa Claus, and he acted like one, too. He had had a career that spanned most of the modern labor movement in the U.S. He went out of his way to meet me many

Phil Mamber

times. "Let's see if we can get you into UE," he told me. "That would be great," I replied. Once again, the problem was the Taft-Hartley Act. "Don't give up. We'll find out what we can do about that," said Phil, and he arranged a meeting with the UE lawyer. But, alas, he couldn't find any way around it either.

So I went back to Rand Wilson at Jobs With Justice. We talked about the idea of starting an independent union. He gave me the names of two lawyers he thought could help us get started.

Rand Wilson, who helped set us on the right path. Several incarnations down the road, he is now working for the Service Employees' Union, SEIU local 888; and is seen here at an SEIU convention.

One of the lawyers was Bob Schwartz, who has written most of the essential works of labor law for union stewards. Bob was happy to help, but he said, "I don't think you want to pay lawyer fees on a regular basis. However, I know an excellent old-time labor consultant, Paul McCarthy, who might be just the man for you guys."

I called Paul on his vacation on Cape Cod. He agreed to see me and Jim Kowalski, our treasurer, at a little Middle Eastern restaurant near the Museum. After talking over lunch, he agreed to work with us on a trial basis. Little did I know that he had serious misgivings based on a tee shirt I was wearing made by my friend Tad Jordan, a silkscreen artist in New Hampshire. It was a takeoff on my name, Raysson, and that I was from California. The tee shirt was a takeoff on a popular ad at the time about California raisins. Well, you can imagine, a caricature of me on the Tee shirt in the form of a raisin from California. "Who is this guy?" thought McCarthy. Somehow, he took the job anyway, even knowing we couldn't pay him for a year until the independent union got established. *If* it got established. Bob Schwartz kindly agreed to come on board for when we needed specialized legal advice.

10

Troubled waters rising, the storm is on its way,
Troubled waters, it might be here today.
--from *Troubled Waters Rising* by Steve Sufet

STEALTH AND SECRECY

All our plans were targeted for the window of opportunity that comes at the end of every contract period. That's the period when the contract is not in effect. Usually both sides will agree to extend that period while negotiating a new contract. But this opening between the past and future contracts can provide an opportunity for union members to withdraw from a union and/or form or join a new one. If *that* happens it is also an opportunity for management to get rid of any union at all. In this case, it ended up as a three-way election in which one could either vote for keeping the old union (UPGWA), bringing in a new independent union, or voting for having no union at all.

Our window opened up in January, 1995.

Lisa Rhea, Dave Hebden and myself and a few other people who had worked so hard to form a union were now working harder to see that our efforts weren't totally lost. Jill Abatemarco had left the Museum by this time. Joe Hodnick, a newcomer, also became one of the primary workers in this cause.

Very carefully, we had gone on a recruiting spree to get a slate of potential officers ready to run for office under what we hoped would be a new union. We tried and I guess succeeded in doing this under the radar. We finally had a full ticket of people ready to run for office when the time came. Our projected candidates came from all segments of the guard force. This was deliberate, so that everyone would feel represented by someone from their community. We stated it this way: "Our candidates represent the diverse backgrounds of our membership, so the issues of one and all of you will be represented and cared for with all fairness and concern."

We even had two candidates from the sizeable immigrant community on the MFA guard force, Semi Ereyo from Africa and Milo Remy from Haiti. Milo Remy had been a student organizer and protester in Haiti. "I have always been interested in workers' issues," said Milo, "defending their rights and improving their working conditions."

The way we had to recruit our candidates and the idea of getting people from all sectors of the guard force had both good and bad points. The main advantage was that everyone on the guard force would hopefully feel represented. The problem, which we found out later, was that we hadn't vetted some of our choices well enough. In time, we discovered that many of them had little idea of or motivation for the effort, passion and personal commitment expected of a union officer. However, given the situation, we were just glad we had them aboard.

Just as when we had first organized our union in 1992, we needed well over fifty percent of the members to sign cards, this time in favor of a new independent union. The need for secrecy was doubled this time. Not only did we need to escape the gaze of management, but even more so, we needed to escape the gaze of the International Union. I knew UPGWA would swoop in to freeze our assets as soon they found out and try to put us in trusteeship under their control. This was, of course, much more difficult now, after UPGWA's horrific betrayal.

When we met in secret, the meeting had to be with our most trusted members: Jim Kowalski, our treasurer, Russell Gilfoy and Joe Hodnick were a few, plus Lisa, Dave and myself. Of course, McCarthy was also in on it. "How are we going to get cards signed so that word doesn't get out?" Lisa asked.

Well, we passed the cards around, and got them signed as close to the time that the window opened up as possible. We did it as quickly as possible. We hoped the prospective candidates would keep quiet, and they did.

In the meantime, we brought in McCarthy, who along with Lisa and me, had a conference with management to see if some compromise on the wage question could be made. Of course, they turned down all our questions, suggestions and possible demands without a second thought. At any rate, it introduced them to McCarthy. They might have wondered about where UPGWA was in all this (they did ask, in passing). But they were all too used to the union leadership's absenteeism. Since we never heard from UPGWA about it, we didn't worry. Moreover, it disguised our real intent, which was to disengage from UPGWA forever and form a new union.

Finally, the window of opportunity did come. The day before, I had Jim Kowalski remove our money to a small bank that only he and I knew about. We left a small stipend to cover any little bit of money UPGWA might spend on our behalf. The very day after we changed banks, and as soon as they heard about our intentions, the International Union made their move. But it was too late.

Below is the first part of a letter from UPGWA, which was the beginning of their desperate attempt to take over the union and stop us from going independent. They also wanted to retrieve all our money and assets. The letter explains what they would attempt to do with us. Fortunately, it didn't work. Our under-the-radar campaign was well underway before they could seize control of our local.

Now we had to wait and see if we had the votes.

International Union, UNITED PLANT GUARD WORKERS OF AMERICA (UPGWA)

INTERNATIONAL HEADQUARTERS: 25510 Kelly Rd., Roseville, Michigan 48066
TELEPHONE: (810) 772-7250 FAX: (810) 772-9644

EUGENE P. McCONVILLE
President

LOUIS R. SCOHY
Vice President

RONALD L. WARFIELD
Secretary Treasurer

January 30, 1995

Mike Raysson, President
Local 541 - UPGWA
308 Brookline St.
Cambridge, MA 02139

Dear Brother Raysson:

It has come to our attention that conditions exist in Local Union No. 541 which seriously impair its ability to perform is functions regarding the property and assets of the Local, to assure the performance of collective bargaining agreements or otherwise to assure carrying out the legitimate objectives of both the International and Local Unions.

Specifically, certain officers and members have initiated action to withdraw and disaffiliate from the International Union, UPGWA. As a consequence, we are compelled to take action to protect the assets of Local Union No. 541.

Pursuant to the authority granted by Article XII, Section 2.(b)(c) and (d)(3) of the International Constitution, we hereby appoint Kerry Lacey as the Administrator of Local Union No. 541 with full power and authority to take all necessary and appropriate action to protect and preserve the property and assets of the Local and its Units, including, but not limited to the suspension of Local or Unit officers, and the custody and control of bank accounts. A copy of the appointment order is enclosed.

In accordance with Article XII, Section 2.(b), the officers of Local No. 541 are being ordered to show cause why they should not be suspended, and why the appointed Administrator should not continue to administer the affairs of the Local. A copy of the Order to Show Cause and Notice of Hearing is enclosed.

Smile, Massachusetts, smile,
Thy virtue still outbraves
The frowns of British Isle
--from *A Song* (1776), anonymously written

ENTER MALCOLM ROGERS

In the summer of 1994, Malcolm Rogers became the new director of the Boston Museum of Fine Arts. His arrival coincided with our last days with UPGWA and the beginnings of our campaign to form a new independent union. Perhaps, the introduction of a new director like Malcolm at just this time was deliberate in the Museum's strategy to get rid of the union and to cut out those employees (or jobs) who didn't fit into the corporate mold. In filling this Machiavellian role as director of the Museum of Fine Arts, Rogers immediately became our main antagonist and the face of the corporate powers who hid behind the scenes. What could be expected from the new director became clear from the beginning, when I tried to introduce him to our consultant, Paul McCarthy, and Malcolm refused to even shake his hand.

The nasty episode early on of museum management reneging on the negotiated pay raise in our original contract—with the underlying suspicion of a collusion between the Museum management and UPGWA—had begun in the spring just prior to Malcolm's arrival. So it seems that Malcolm's entrance at that time and place was orchestrated, among other things, to successfully bring that agenda to fruition.

When the case of the reneged contract morphed into our campaign to introduce an independent union, Malcolm entered directly into the fray. He became a central figure in the mandatory assemblies which management put on to tell workers why it was against their best interests to start a union and why it was in their best interests to trust in management. The Museum exerted all possible energy to see that no further union presence would exist in the MFA, and so did Malcolm Rogers. He was totally engaged in this effort from the very beginning to the very end, when members of the guard force went to the ballot box to decide whether or not we wanted a labor union to continue to represent us. Yes, Malcolm watched from just beyond the ballot box, staying to the very end. He stared intently as each guard voted, until all the ballots were counted and the independent union had won.

At that same time, Malcolm Rogers put a huge restructuring of the Museum into action. First and foremost, that meant the elimination of eighty-three jobs. If we see a consistent strategy to put in place the corporate vision, then we can understand, perhaps, why Malcolm

Rogers was hired in the summer of 1994 to be the director of the Boston Museum of Fine Arts.

Malcolm was indeed a most unlikely pick to head one of the world's great encyclopedic Art Museums. Up to that moment, his most relevant previous job had been as assistant director of the National Portrait Gallery, London, which highlighted second-rate paintings of great people. By his own admission, he had been highly desirous of the director's position there [See Patti Hartigan, *Malcolm Rogers has left the Building,* Boston Magazine, p. 92, September, 2015.], but he was passed over by the higher-ups.

So why was this Brit, who had none of the experience necessary, either with managing people or dealing with world-class art, chosen to run a Museum like the Boston Museum of Fine Arts? A good guess is that he possessed the exact qualities the corporate powers were looking for to help change the Boston Museum into the corporate mold. That is, he was a charismatic schmoozer and fundraiser, a willing executor of bottom line corporate policies and someone who could remake the Museum into the capitalistic mode of a profitable and going concern.

12

Don't count me out
When I'm on the floor
We'll win again
We've won before
--from *We Belong to the Union (You Can't Break Me)*
by Tim O'Brien

THE WINDOW OF OPPORTUNITY

The window of opportunity had arrived and I felt pretty confident: just an eternal optimist, I guess. Anyone else looking at our situation solely from a rational and logical point of view would have come to the conclusion that we were pretty much doomed. On the one hand, a powerful International Union with tremendous resources and few moral compunctions was moving in to take over our local and remove all power from our hands. On the other hand, one of the most powerful cultural institutions in New England was putting together the final parts of its campaign to rid itself, once and for all, of a very bothersome union.

The Museum management, of course, had their union busters and their corporate lawyers in place again. They did not intend to lose a second time. They seemed to have the advantage right off the bat, because they could say, "See what happened when you got a union!" They ignored the fact that our woes were brought on by them. But it reflected the mentality of a bully, jeering at a weaker opponent.

The other bully, UPGWA, had not given us up for lost. Their main strategy was to blame the problems on me and other leaders. "This is all because you had people like Michael Raysson as leaders! Let us take over and everything will be all right again."

To make things worse, now that the contract was no longer in effect, the Museum did not have to collect dues for us. Collection of union dues by management is one part of the contractual agreement that they no longer had to carry out.

Logistically, it suddenly became tremendously difficult to collect enough money to keep things going for us, what with all the different hours and all the different shifts that guards worked. And add to this the fact that many people just didn't want to pay up. Our guys and gals who went around trying to collect were heroic. Jim Kowalski complained that it was worse than pulling teeth. Russell Gilfoy volunteered, but only if he got those members who actually wanted to pay. Dave Hebden took a somewhat cynical (or realistic) view, based on the seeming impossibility of this undertaking. Dave was convinced that most of the guards would refuse to pay their dues, but he still managed to get a few of the difficult people to pay.

Joe Hodnick was the absolute best, doing the lion's share, for which he deserved a medal.

Then an amazing thing happened. Suddenly, UPGWA stopped their assault. It was not clear why, but it seems that many members of the International Union were not only dissatisfied with the president of UPGWA, Eugene McConville, and some of his lieutenants (Kerry Lacey probably among them), but were also suspicious of their conduct in relation to the handling of union funds. The accusations appeared to be quite serious—serious enough that they were now trying to save their jobs, their reputations and, perhaps, their ability to stay out of jail. Suddenly, Raysson and the Boston Museum of Fine Arts union, local 541, were no longer important.

Now it was just us and the Museum. This was a more manageable fight, one in which I felt we actually had the upper hand. Or as they say, "If we played our cards right."

13

Dump the bosses off our backs, don't listen to their lies
Solidarity Forever means don't mourn—organize![1]

--from *Got My Union* by Steve Suffett

PLAYING OUR CARDS

Joe Hill is one of the patron saints of union organizing. His songs are sung even now by laborers all over the world. He worked with the IWW, The International Workers of the World in the early twentieth century when workers in America were often in dire straits. At that time, Management would go to any extreme including murder to stop organizing laborers. In fact, Joe himself was murdered by firing squad for a crime he did not commit. Shortly before he was executed, Joe sent a letter to his friend and co-worker in the IWW, Big Bill Barnett, in which he exhorted, "Don't mourn for me—organize!" This is what Steve Suffet is referring to in the quote above. It certainly fitted our situation.

Museum management now took up the fight...with a vengeance. They did the things they do, handing out leaflets, holding forced assemblies, sending supervisors around assaulting the guards with management propaganda, and keeping track of "for," "against," and "maybe." The message that they were giving out was that unionizing only made things worse. Inevitably. "You saw what happened when you formed a union. Work with management, don't cause trouble and you'll be all right." Their idea was to cow the people, the guards, into giving up their power, and to bring power back to where it rightfully belonged—with the boss.

It was our job, as I saw it, to sell the guards on themselves, and that "ourselves all together" were the superior force and the better force. Our mission was to place the blame for the betrayal of the guards onto UPGWA, which had not only failed to defend us, but compounded their crime as our Union protectors by siding with management. We had to convince our members that the problem was not a Union, but the *type of Union*, and that a new and independent union was in our best interests and was what we really needed.

For one thing, management had callously taken away our rightly earned pay raises, and for another, the UPGWA had refused to help us in our time of need. But the UPGWA's even more heinous "crime" had been to actually back up management instead of us. We *had* to convince the rank and file to believe that the formation of a new and independent union was in our best interests.

So we appointed communicating stewards. Each steward had a certain number of specific guards to give our side of the story to, and to find out where the guards were at as far as the union was concerned. Then it was the steward's job to ask them what they liked and what they didn't like. It didn't work perfectly, but it worked well enough that we had a pretty good idea of where our members stood.

It helped to have our prospective candidates also ready to introduce themselves and talk to the guards. Since they came from all the different segments of the guard force, we hoped that together they could cover a very wide demographic. Even the fact that we were collecting dues by hand came to our advantage, as this in itself enabled us to communicate with all our members in a more intimate, "person-to-person" way and to share the hardships of members who had little ready cash. The fact that many of them were desperately trying to get by from week to week, and that we were all in the exact same predicament actually created a lot of sympathy and empathy. They could relate to that:

Dues collector: Hi H_____, it's time for dues collection.

H: I'd love to pay you but I'm hard up for cash.

DC: I really understand, H_____, actually we're in the same position

H: Gee, I'm sorry. Maybe I could pay half now...

DC: Thanks. That would be great. How do you feel about our new Union, are you for it?

H: I like the idea, but how do you know the same thing won't happen as last time?

DC: We are rid of those guys! This time it'll be more our own union. We won't let that happen again.

H: Can you promise that?

DC: We'll promise to do everything possible to have your back–and you know you can trust us more that management.

H: That's for sure. Yeah, I think I'm with you.

So unintentionally, the Museum had pushed our communication with our members to a level that was far beyond our ordinary capabilities. The poor dues collection team, which was almost constantly doing their job, gave us the third prong, along with the communicating stewards and prospective officers, in what was a hugely successful communicating system, in spite of all its flaws and difficulties.

Certainly, we would never have planned to do it that way.

When it came down to the final days of the campaign, and the Museum was doing its full court pressure thing, our guys were also going around like crazy. And since management had deliberately forced us into that position, they couldn't complain or try to discipline those people.

In the end, everyone was there for the vote. All the union people, if they were not on a work shift, were there, holding hands. We had worked our butts off. This was the last chance for us. We all stood together on one side of the room. Lisa Rhea was there, along with her half-sister, Brenda Lee. Dave Hebden was there. Russell Gilfoy, Jim Kowalski and Joe Hodnick were there. Various others came in and out when they could, according to their work duties. And, oh yes, I was there.

For the Museum, there was Dave Moffatt. He was the Museum manager who was put in charge of the campaign against us in the latter stages of 1994. He had also been one of the brains behind the idea for the Museum to renege on our negotiated pay raise. And he continued right to the end as a heavyweight in the campaign to rid the Boston Museum of Fine Arts of a labor union.

Malcolm Rogers, the new Director of the Museum, was there. He had taken an extremely active part in the "*rid the Museum of the union*" campaign, including the forced assemblies and the go rounds. Gail Mallard, head of human resources was there. Usually she was a somewhat dark, distant and foreboding character. We called

On April 3, 1995, we received the National Labor Relations Board official certification declaring MISU the winner in the three-way election.

FORM NLRB-4279 (2-88)

UNITED STATES OF AMERICA
NATIONAL LABOR RELATIONS BOARD

RC — RM — RD

MUSEUM OF FINE ARTS

Employer

and

MFA INDEPENDENT SECURITY UNION

Petitioner

and

INTERNATIONAL UNION, UNITED PLANT GUARD WORKERS OF AMERICA (UPGWA) and its LOCAL NO. 541

Intervenor

TYPE OF ELECTION (CHECK ONE)

☐ CONSENT
☒ STIPULATED
☐ RD DIRECTED
☐ BOARD DIRECTED

(ALSO CHECK BOX BELOW WHEN APPROPRIATE)

☐ 8(b)(7)

CASE 1-RC-20248

CERTIFICATION OF REPRESENTATIVE

An election has been conducted under the Board's Rules and Regulations. The Tally of Ballots shows that a collective-bargaining representative has been selected. No timely objections have been filed.

As authorized by the National Labor Relations Board, it is certified that a majority of the valid ballots have been cast for

MFA INDEPENDENT SECURITY UNION

and that it is the exclusive collective-bargaining representative of the employees in the following appropriate unit.

UNIT:

All full-time and regular part-time watch guards, security guards, parking lot guards, and security receptionists employed by the Employer at its Boston location, but excluding the Director of Protective Services, the Assistant Director of Protective Services, the Secretary of Protective Services, admissions cashiers, control center operators, cleaning guards, night supervisors, day supervisors, evening supervisors, all other employees, and all other supervisors as defined in the Act.

Signed at Boston, Massachusetts

On the 3rd day of April 1995

/s/ Roy M. Schoenfeld

Acting Regional Director, Region One
National Labor Relations Board

her the "Dark Queen." But lately she had become smiling and friendly, talking to everyone and attempting to bring recalcitrant guards back into the fold.

Both sides stood around as the voters entered the booth, one by one. Finally, the end time came. Voting was over. Now the counting began.

The first time had been easy for us, winning by a landslide. This time, it was closer. Much closer. First it would surge one way, then the other. When it was almost over, it was still in doubt. Then one, two, three, four, five, six, seven...yes! yes! We had won *by seven votes*. Four votes in the other direction and we would have lost. Nevertheless, we were ecstatic! On management's side, they were crushed. The campaign to rid the Museum of a labor union had failed again!

Malcolm Roger stormed out. Gail Mallard cried. Dave Moffatt just looked stunned. Well, he should have been, for a few days later, he lost his job. We hugged and kissed and clapped and stamped and screamed for joy.

14

What does the workman want?
He wants fair play and equal rights
And equal chance for all.
--from *The Workman's Square Deal*, anonymous

MISU'S FIRST CONTRACT CAMPAIGN

After Dave Moffatt got fired, I approached him with the idea that he just might like to reveal some information. I asked him, "Dave, what can you tell me about the Museum's contingency plans in case we won?" "We had none," said Dave. It took a little while for me to understand that the Museum just didn't believe we had a chance in hell to succeed.

I asked McCarthy about it. "Is it true, Paul, that no one would ever expect us to win?" "That's right", he answered. "In that situation, unions never win." I was shocked. "You knew that?" "Yes."

Anyway, since we had won, the time was near for negotiations. But first we had a contest to name the new independent union. We had a meeting and there really was a fun time tossing names around the room. I forget who came up with the winning idea. I know my idea lost. The winner was Museum Independent Security Union. MISU.

With such a close election, management was going to be much tougher than usual, and negotiations are always tough. Because they knew the bargaining unit was divided, the Museum had increased leverage. And they were mad as hell at losing. So they started out by offering us a paltry raise of five cents.

It was not necessarily a good strategy, because it got our people pissed off—and motivated—in return.

This was our response:

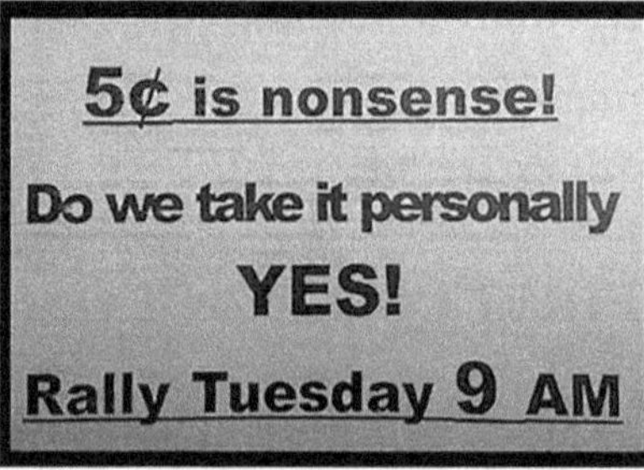

In response to our rally and to the widespread anger over the paltry, insulting raise management offered, they generously raised it to eight cents. This was just what we needed. When the members heard about it, they were even more incensed. First an old guard of Swedish descent, Carl Berglund, came up with the slogan, "Five cents is nonsense," then "Eight cents is nonsense!" And he, an artist himself, drew a cartoon to go along with it called *Attack on Eight Penny Castle, AD 1995*. Everyone was up in arms, ready to demonstrate. The MFA had mobilized the troops for us.

This was also our first negotiation with Paul McCarthy as our negotiator. He ran a very tight ship and was kind of an anti-UPGWA. He made it clear that we had to concentrate on our main issues and that we had to be sure that that was what the members wanted. Our negotiating team back then was made up of Donald Cusack, Katie O'Brien, Russell Gilfoy, Jim Kowalski, John Storrow, Lisa Rhea and myself.

McCarthy made it clear that he was to be the one who did the talking to management, but he made sure we had plenty of caucuses to let him know where we were at. If we wanted to say anything during the actual negotiating sessions, we had to pass him a piece of paper with a message on it. But the absolute main thing we learned from him was this: *our demonstrations with the public and rallies and communications with our members were where the negotiations would be won or lost.* [Chapter 25, on *Negotiations* gives a much more detailed account of what negotiations entail.]

Contract campaigns are always difficult, but this, our first as an independent union, was especially difficult. Until we came to an agreement in the negotiations, we had to continue to collect dues by hand instead of by automatic deductions. I have already stated how difficult this was. Joe Hodnick and I did most of the collecting. But it was an additional chance to communicate with the members. It works, though I don't recommend it.

Those members of the bargaining team who were seeing for the first time what it was like sitting in the same room with management and attempting to negotiate with them were taken aback by the cold and inhuman attitude of their representatives at the bargaining table. Lisa and I had seen it all before, but it is something you never quite get over.

One time Katie Getchell, the Museum's deputy director for curatorial administration, came to a negotiating meeting. She was famous for giving guards a hard time for nit picking offenses, like being a few feet outside their assigned gallery. She accused guards of being lazy and inefficient. We read her quote after quote from patrons of the Museum who had signed our petition and had praised the guards to the skies for their service and knowledge, and, in addition, how much we meant to them as part of their Museum experience. "Well," said Katie, "We get lots of negative comments from visitors about guards." "Can you tell us some?" we asked. "Why yes," said Katie huffily. "There was a visitor who complained about a guard yawning at the door." We were dumbfounded. "Is that it?" Apparently it was, because she had nothing more to say on the subject.

The bargaining team for management was usually made up of their lawyer, Scott Faust, his assistant, the head of human resources, her assistant and the head of security. The head of human resources, depending on the time frame, was known as either the "Dark queen 1" or the "Dark Queen 2". They earned those names well. The lawyer, Faust, seemed like he may have once been a nice guy, but he also earned his name well. The head of security, whoever that was at the time, rarely talked except to explain some fine point. If we got a good contract, they were fired. So we shouldn't have been surprised about them. But when they introduced themselves, they actually seemed, for a moment, like good people. Then the bargaining session completely erased any semblance of that first impression.

McCarthy's dictum—that nothing is won at the table and everything is won outside on the streets and in communicating with our fellow workers in the workplace—gave us hope. So the members of the bargaining team also became regulars at those rallies and demonstrations. They talked to the other guards. They were always at the Union meetings, where we tried to let members know what progress was being made. Afterward, we encouraged those who came to the rallies and meetings to spread the word to others.

The worst thing that can happen is that the other members think you are hiding things from them.

Thankfully, we were able to motivate guards to come out to the demonstrations that we now regularly were putting on, so they could express their displeasure by picketing and leafleting. This was the campaign where we first learned the value of reaching out to the outside public and the media. Guards would often come out to weekday demonstrations during their lunch and coffee breaks. Then we would greet each other and have a little welcome conversation while we were passing out our leaflets. It was a great way to break people into the empowerment of leafleting to the public. Sometimes the guards could get into conversations with the Museum patrons, too.

It was also when we first put requests on the leaflets that we handed out for patrons to call in to the Museum and let management know how they, the public, felt about the Museum's treatment of their low-paid workers. And this worked in spades, as the Museum was flooded with calls

Management likes to draw negotiations out as long as possible to tire out union members who are demonstrating outside. But it seemed they were just as anxious as we were—probably more—to get it over with. They were getting worn out answering those phone calls from the public. And that is how we wanted it. The two ways, and only ways, I had of judging where we were at in negotiations were: How anxious management appeared to be to get it over with, and How anxious our own people appeared to be to get it over with.

Part of one of our first leaflets,
encouraging the public to call in to Museum management

As hard-working, low-wage earners, and family people, we are distressed at the MFA's lack of concern for its employees, regardless of how large their profits are.

We, who have devoted ourselves to the MFA's aims and traditions find ourselves dismayed by the corporate philosophy which now dominates their leadership.

We are asking you to show your concern by calling Malcolm Rogers, director of the MFA, at (617) 369-3200 to encourage him to negotiate a fair contract with us!

Please note that it is not our intention to discourage you from visiting and enjoying the Museum. We look forward to serving you. Have a wonderful time and please come again!

Thank you for your kind support on our behalf.

Katie O'Brien was a young woman in her twenties who broke into union activism during the campaign for an independent union and later in negotiations. In 1998, she became Union Vice President. She had this to say about her experiences in helping to form MISU and then working on the contract: "...I have found out that working with MISU (Museum Independent Security Union) has been one of the outstanding experiences of my life... My union experiences began with our successful struggle to become an independent union, through picketing, leafleting and attending countless meetings."

In the end, we did get good raises, salaries and benefits. In fact, many larger unions told me personally that they were amazed we had gotten such a good contract. But management was able to put in some difficult wording. The coup de grace was Malcolm Roger's insistence on giving all guards the voluntary choice of joining the union—or not. This insidious strategy, deceptively called an "open shop," is often used by management to bust a union.

In an "open shop," a person can refuse to join the union, pay no dues, but still get the exact same benefits as those workers who do pay dues. It is like paying little or no taxes but getting the same benefits as those who do, like what many of the rich people in our country are able to get away with: and it is just as insidious as that.

We managed to change that clause so that it only applied to guards who were already employed by the Museum. New guards would automatically join the union. While this seemed to be somewhat devastating, in the end (like hand collecting dues) it was extremely helpful. It forced us to become an even better union, because it forced us to explain to every guard why they should join. Plus, our people noticed how hard we were working to make the union represent the rank and file.

Surprisingly, most guards chose to join. In the months to come, we supplied such good service, especially in grievances. In the end, only three or four of our old guards didn't join the union.

15

Come all of you good workers, good news to you I'll tell
Of how that good old union has come in here to dwell.

--from *Which Side Are You On?*
by Florence Patton Reece

THE MUSEUM INDEPENDENT SECURITY UNION

Most of the candidates on our ticket, which we called simply, "The Progressive Ticket," went on to win their leadership positions in the new union, including myself. Things started off in a refreshing way. The most important officers of MISU were the stewards. Together we vowed to investigate and fight, if there were any grounds at all for fighting, each and every grievance.

The reasoning behind making the grievance procedure such a central point in how our union worked was two-fold. First, we wanted all guards to know we had their back. Second, we learned an important point in the justice system, which is that each case can set a precedent for future cases. If you don't defend one case, then that can weaken your defense on the next case. And we tried to make sure that our stewards would be absolutely impartial in conducting a case, whether they liked the person they were representing or not. If that was too hard for any steward, we would get another steward to represent the disciplined guard.

Looking back, I think it was our insistence on backing all guards, except in the most obvious cases of guilt, that won over the new union in the minds of our members. In many ways having an independent union was a godsend. It enabled us to have autonomy unheard of with UPGWA—and probably with most AFL-CIO local unions also. We learned the old-fashioned way, by trial and error.

Having Paul McCarthy and Robert Schwartz working with us was equally important. McCarthy was pragmatic. He had been through what we were going through many times before. Paul preferred to resolve things on the human level and on the strategic level, if possible, rather than the legal one. The fact is that the playing field of the law is heavily slanted toward management in labor-management disputes, as it is in most other areas of working life.

Talking with McCarthy, I learned the joy of strategizing and positioning. He would always bring up the old dictum: "It's not what you have, but what they think you have." He loved Sun-Tzu, the famous Chinese author of the "Art of War." Paul would extol winning battles without actually going to war.

On the other hand, if it did come down to the fine points of legal procedure, Schwartz was there. As I have said, he wrote the books that were and are considered the Bible for union stewards. Of course, if I called him I had to be as brief and as quick as possible, because I was immediately on his clock and he let me know it. "Five minutes and counting..."

Most people have a very practical view of a labor union: "Is it helping me *personally*?" Not only in terms of wages, but in everyday life at work people wonder, *Is the union there to help me when I need it?* One of the most amazing examples of this was Don Cusack. He probably hadn't even voted for the union in the election. Soon after the election was over, Don out and out told me he was not going to join, not after what had happened. Then he made a request. "Listen, if you can get management to do 'such and such a thing, then I'll join your union!"

As I remember, the issue was that Don had some very special health concerns in his family, which called for him to come home and attend to those at special times. So far, the Museum had refused permission for him to do so and Don was very upset about that.

It so happened that that very day I went to management and somehow convinced them to let Don have permission to do that very thing. Of course, the first thing I did after that was to go to Don and tell him.

"Well I got you that time off for your family!"

"I don't believe you!" says Don.

When I finally convinced him he, being a man of his word, immediately joined up. He was one of our best unionists. He became an officer in due course and worked on our bargaining teams. Don had been a counselor and student advisor in one of the local school systems. He became a kind of *eminence grise* for us, giving a much-needed mature perspective coming from long experience, sensibility and empathy.

In a relatively short time, MISU became a solid organization. I talked to many people from other unions and it didn't seem that any of them had stewards or a grievance team like ours. There was no longer any question of a divided membership. Almost everyone was a union member, and voluntarily and enthusiastically so.

It looked like smooth sailing for our fledgling independent union. I mean, we were masters of our own fate, so what could possibly go wrong?

16

There's trouble fast approaching
And the skies are overcast
But let us not lose sight of
All the lessons of the past
--from Stand Together by Bernard Carney

CIVIL WAR

I have said that our candidates for office in the beginning of our new independent union were most helpful in our campaign with management and UPGWA. But there was a problem we didn't foresee. After some months had passed and things had settled down, many of the new officers—with the exception of our stewards—did not seem to understand the importance of fulfilling their official duties. Most of these people took it easy and neglected their union work. This included missing all of our executive board meetings.

All union officers are expected to attend each executive board meeting if possible. Many of the initiatives in running union affairs begin there, and it is important that this is a democratic process that includes as many people as possible. I remember that when I was hot to get my ideas in action as union president, McCarthy would counsel me to get the full executive board behind them.

Nevertheless, those of us who did attend would go around to apprise these other officers of what had gone down at the meetings. We would also show them the minutes from the meeting. But the minutes generally just contained short summaries of the major events on the agenda. This was not enough for them. They wanted an in-depth written report which they could go over at their leisure.

There is a big problem in writing down detailed reports of executive union meetings. It is not just the extra work in writing and passing out detailed reports. There is the chance that such in-depth reports somehow got into the hands of management, and that could seriously compromise the union and its members in a host of worrisome and possibly vital ways.

We told the union officers if they wanted to know everything that went on at the executive meeting, they needed to come to the damn meetings. That pissed them off.

Suddenly the success and solidarity of our new union was being put to an extreme test, not by management but from within. McCarthy often told me, "Even more than management, you'll often find it's your own people who give you the most trouble!" Since a majority of those dissident officers were minorities or people of color, the whole thing took on a racist tinge. At least, they saw it that way.

For me, I was slow to acknowledge, or even to understand, that maybe I wasn't as sensitive/aware of the need to bridge the gap between the white workers who attended the executive meetings and the black members, who seemed to feel unwelcome.

Finally, we had a war on our hands. And it was at this point that a young African-American, Anthony Meikle, stepped forward. Anthony was a young man with a large imagination, but who had not yet been able to find his place in life. He would get excited about things and we would hear him in the locker room go, "Wow, Flippin this!" and, "Flippin that!" ("Flippin" was his word for things that seemed strange or wonderful to him, and there were many things that did.) He lived in a world that was filled with wonder, and somehow, this union situation brought his underlying abilities into the fore.

Anthony was extremely quirky and generally had little to do with union affairs. He came up to me. "Raysson, let me take care of this." He proposed a meeting of the two sides in which he would work as moderator and facilitator. Somehow, it seemed like a good idea to me. "Go for it, Anthony." Since he was black, the dissidents had no trouble approving him. And because he was neutral, we also approved.

Anthony was amazing. He very carefully let both groups explain their issues and made sure they were heard by the other side. In the end, his decision was that we should apologize to the dissidents. I remember Joe Hodnick whispering to me, "Michael, just grit your teeth and go along with it. Everything will turn out all right."

And it did! Anthony's work, which came at such a critical juncture in our history, was pure genius. I learned a lot about apologies and forgiveness. And that really was all they wanted.

Things mostly returned to normal and the work got done, although at the next election, most of the officers who were very discontented did not run again. They were fully assuaged by our apologies, and several workers of color did continue in the steward and union officer mix. I did not talk to the others, but I would guess that they had enough of being an officer, and they did continue to participate in union affairs. Anthony Meikle, although he never became an officer, contributed regularly to the Union Newsletter.

The people who did run turned out to be diligent and enthusiastic.

This episode helped us to realize the need for better communications with all our people. One thing which really helped was our newsletter which we put out regularly and which contained contributions from any member who cared to do so, including a page or two of guard artwork. Anthony, I must report, was one such contributor. We will say more about this later.

17

We need truths in their wild state,
insurrectionary beauty
that excites our curiosity,
outrageous goodness
that drives us to perform
--from This Is a Perfect Moment by Rob Brezsney--

JOSH LYONS

In 1996, something happened that, at least in my experience, was very special and one-time only. A young kid by the name of Josh Lyons was hired as a guard. He had a genius for union work and made a huge and indelible imprint. At first, he was just *too* smart. He was also much too far to the left for most of the guard force. But he was immediately interested in the union and he had great ideas.

It was a culture shock for both Josh and for some of the old-time guards. The radical culture he was used to had little in the way of restrictions. A young newcomer like himself was welcomed into that milieu and encouraged to contribute both his ideas and his youthful energy at the disposal of the cause. So he naturally jumped into the union "cause" with exuberance and a plethora of ideas. Some people have thought he was pushy, but he was not like that at all, he was just being himself.

Most of the guards were just not like that. They were infinitely more conservative, even the liberal ones. There was a tradition and there were unspoken restrictions, and, of course, many of the guards were from New England, a bastion of circumspection and reserve.

So it was that he stepped on many toes of those who had been at the Museum well before he arrived, just by being himself. He paid for that and he learned. Lisa Rhea was vice president at the time. She hung out a lot with Jerome Ware, who was our sergeant-at-arms. Somewhere, Lisa had picked up the idea that there was a strict and proper decorum that a new guard should observe as they advanced up the Union Ladder.

Lisa being an avid sports fan may have gotten this idea from the treatment given rookies by the more experienced old-time players. This is a time-honored tradition on almost all sports teams. The young players are expected to be extremely respectful to the veterans and accept a subservient role at first, till they are thought to have "paid their dues". Of course, this could also come from African culture, which may have resonated in Lisa's familial upbringing, reflecting extreme respect for one's elders. Jerome was also extremely respectful to his elders, addressing all elderly women, *"Honey"* or *"Dear."*

"That young dude has got to learn the ropes and pay his dues before he gets my respect," Lisa told me. Jerome pretty much followed her lead and they put poor Josh through his paces. It was painful to watch and often Josh would be close to tears. More than once, Lisa said to Josh, "Watch out young man or I'll get your ass kicked out of the Union!" Lisa didn't mean it, really. It was actually good-natured trash talk (well, mostly). But Josh didn't know that. "Can she really do that?" he asked me.

I took Josh aside and said, "Look, you're okay, but you've gotta understand where Lisa and Jerome are coming from. They expect you to act like the rookie on the sports team. And you have to do that. They'll come around if you do."

And they did. Gradually, he was accepted. Originally, I hadn't thought that he had much in people skills. But later, as I went around the Museum, I would even see many guards, often people of color, hugging him with large smiles on their faces. When he became a Union officer, he got the highest percentage of the popular vote in our history. And he and Lisa and Jerome became fast friends.

I am relating this not only as an instructive tale of a young man learning how to fit into a union, but also because this injection of progressive and even radical thinking marked an unprecedented and positive addition into our budding union. His contributions opened up huge amounts of new ground which became part of our modus operandi in the future, even after he left. This contribution was marked through and through with his extreme intelligence and his genuine elan.

After a while, he took charge of our newsletter. He had a stream of great ideas on that. He gussied it up, and even added news from other labor unions, locally and around the country. He decorated it with beautiful typography and borders from William Morris. (Morris was the leading exponent of the English Arts and Crafts Movement in the nineteenth century. That he was an ardent socialist probably endeared him to Josh.)

At length he had our little newsletter (called the *Security Blanket)* looking like a work of art. He kept impeccable records and gathered invaluable intelligence, both in house and out. He was at all our demonstrations and even reached out to other organizations and got them to come. And so on.

I had hoped that Josh would take up a career as a grassroots union organizer. But that was not to be. Alas,

A sample of Josh's newsletter pages.

Design by William Morris

Striking French Museum Guards Close Louvre

Preface by Michael Raysson

As Museum guards, we found the following event, which occurred in May, extremely interesting. First of all, be cause it involved our counterparts in the greatest museum in Europe–the security guards of the Louvre. Second, because it graphically shows the difference between the power of unions in Europe and the U.S.

Amazingly, the striking watchguards were able to completely shutdown the Louvre for almost an entire week–representing the loss of about 100,000 visitors!

. . . .

PARIS (AP) The Louvre opened its doors for the first time in five days Monday, (5-26-97) after striking night watchmen agreed to end their blockade of entrances to France's largest museum, a Louvre spokeswoman said.

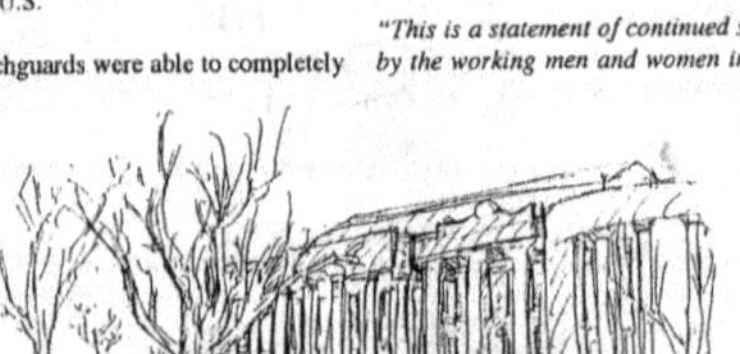

Drawing by James Kowalski

The watchmen, protesting working conditions, blocked the glass pyramid entrance in the main courtyard of the Louvre. Tourists had been shut out since Thursday from seeing the Mona Lisa and the thousands of other artworks and antiquities at the Louvre, which usually attracts 20,000 visitors a day this time of year.

The Louvre opened at 2 P.M.. (1200 GMT) after the strikers agreed to open new negotiations with the museum's management, Louvre spokeswoman Patricia Mounier said.

The roughly 100 guards on strike were protesting personnel cuts, complaints about their uniforms and a loss of vacation time to compensate for night shifts.

60,000 March in Solidarity with Detroit Newspaper Workers

On Saturday, June 21st, an estimated 60,000 union members from across the country marched in solidarity with the 2,000 Detroit newspaper workers who have been on strike for over two years.

"This is a statement of continued solidarity and commitment by the working men and women in this country," said AFL-CIO President John Sweeney at the start of the march outside Tiger Stadium.

Chanting *"Hey, ho, scab labor has got to go!"* and *"Knight-Ridder, Gannett, the fight ain't over yet!,"* marchers rallied in front of the offices of The Detroit News and Free Press, demanding an end to union-busting and a just union contract. Some marchers shook their fists and made obscene gestures at the scabs watching from the Detroit News building. Others yelled "Jump! Jump!" The scabs could not be reached for comment.

Judge Thomas Wilks ruled Friday that the strike was caused by unfair labor practices. He ruled that the Free Press and The Detroit News must take back as many as 1,100 workers even if it means displacing the scabs.

As one striker said, *"We need the community to remember that our struggle is not over and that we still need to have our jobs back, and most importantly we need contracts."*

For more information on how you can help, please call Jobs with Justice at 617-491-2525.

Page 8, Security Blanket, June 1997

he went on to the London School of Economics. Presently he is on the satellite team at Human Rights Watch.

Unfortunately, we don't have any pictures of Josh in our archives. But this is a mug shot of him from Human Rights Watch. He hasn't changed that much.

Recently I was vividly reminded of an important connection with Josh that I had forgotten: I found this very significant statement by Josh among my union memorabilia this evening:

"My first contact with MISU was at a Jobs with Justice meeting in January, 1996. This strange man we had never seen before introduced himself as the "President of MISU" and explained that the MFA security guards were fighting for their first contract but were under attack from management. He then asked for our support at a Martin Luther King Day rally in front of the Museum. Needless to say, we were excited about helping and we mobilized people for the rally. The day was bitterly cold and windy, which made our job of talking with visitors and passing out leaflets especially difficult. But what I remember about that day was the incredible happiness and warmth from the guards who were with us on the line. Although we didn't know each other, I think we shared, if only for that day, a special bond of friendship and trust. It was a real example of solidarity in action, which I can only describe as a kind of "union high." After the rally, several members of Jobs with Justice received cards in the mail, thanking us for our support, and I remember how touched I was to receive one. Michael came to the next Jobs with Justice meeting and announced to thunderous applause that MISU had won a great contract. I was honored to help in this little way, and I have been honored to work with MISU ever since as a proud member."

Much later, while he was at Human Rights Watch, Josh told me some wildly hilarious stories about the time he returned to the USA after going to the London School of Economics. He was desperate for a job and somehow he wangled a gig in the upper echelons of a far right wing organization, where he was awarded the highest security clearance. Josh was so far left that he was able to honestly tell them, "I promise that I will never, ever vote for a Democrat!"

I'm a modern chief executive, I wear a pin-striped suit I'm full of deep compassion, when I give someone the boot.

--from I'm a Modern Chief Executive by Jim Lesses

THE BOSTON MASSACRE

In 1999, about seven years after organizing a union under UPGWA and four years after reorganizing with MISU, the fateful event at the Museum which became known as The Boston Massacre exploded in our union like a bomb. The name for this corporate coup, "The Boston Massacre," came from an editorial in the Art Newspaper of September, 1999, by Anna Somers Cocks.

When the corporate Museum in its incarnation at the Boston Museum of Fine Arts was ready for a Coup d'etat, they struck swiftly.

First off, they put a solid majority in place on the Board of Trustees. Most all of the old-timers were gone, replaced one by one by their corporate counterparts. According to *Deborah Weisgall, (Pop Goes the Museum, p. 117, Boston Magazine, October, 1995),* the Museum's Board of Trustees was becoming practically a club for high-end investment advisors.

"They understand money," an elderly patron confided in me. "There's been a shift from the benevolent old Boston patron to a much more active management," said one recently appointed trustee. Alan Strassman, currently the president emeritus of the board of trustees, is a founder of Martingale Asset Management. He was for years CEO of Batterymarch Financial Management and began his career working for George Putnam, who once managed Harvard's endowment, among other large chunks of capital. The economist Kate Feldstein and Peter Lynch, Fidelity Investment's superstar, were trustees. Ned Johnson III the CEO of Fidelity, a long-time trustee, is now an honorary one; but his wife, Lillie, is on the board, as is Thomas H. Lee, of Snapple deal fame. "These are people who have made their fortunes and want to see a return on them."

They had learned from their past mistakes in handling the security guards. I believe, in their mind, the main mistake was in not getting rid of potential ringleaders.

Certainly, that's what they did on the fateful day of June 25, 1999.

In a surprise attack, *with one quick strike the Museum terminated* almost all of the most independent thinkers and leaders in the curatorial department. Foremost was Jonathan Fairbanks, head and creator of the American Decorative Arts Department, which he had started over thirty years before. He was more or less the leader of all the other curators and worked as an intermediary between the administration and the curatorial staff whenever any grievances came up between the two. Jonathan was physically led out of the Museum by the assistant director of security. I'm glad it wasn't a guard. The key to his office was taken away. Several other "troublemakers" were likewise fired and put out on the streets. Most notable (and, perhaps, notorious) was the venerable Anne Poulet, the longtime curator of European Decorative Arts.

It was a sweeping and well-executed purge.

Ted Stebbins, a longtime curator of American Painting at the Museum, who had been promoted in the aftermath of the massacre to the chair of the newly named "Art of the Americas," wasn't fired, but he resigned angrily a few months later. He and his lawyer handed a letter of condemnation to Rogers. "It was a wounding of the curatorial staff who he said were treated like criminals," reported Patti Hartigan *(Malcolm Rogers has Left the Building, Boston Magazine, p. 95, September, 2015).*

The curators were told that their positions were abolished by a vote of the Board of Trustees, although at least one assistant, Jeff Munger of European Decorative Arts, was soon after offered the head curator's job. He declined and left. Other trustees, not on the board, didn't find out until afterwards. Many of them were furious. However, one unidentified board member responded to questions on the Massacre by saying that Museum Director, Malcolm Rogers, had "done a great job bringing in money and getting people into the restaurant and the shop." [Beacon Hill/Back Bay Chronicle, August 31, 1999 and Observer.com (online), *Malcolm Rogers talks Smugly After Boston Massacre.]*

This was pretty much the first takeover of a Museum institution by corporate powers. The rest of the museum world, the academic and scholarly world and the art world were up in arms about it. Criticism rained down from all quarters.

In my fury I imagined Malcolm Rogers being in a huge cesspool, with only his nose above it. Sixteen years later, almost all the Museums and cultural institutions have had their own takeovers. The Boston Museum of Fine Arts set the tone. Now, everyone has pretty much accepted this as status quo.

Voices in opposition

Extracts from the more than 100 letters sent to the Museum of Fine Arts

HAM-FISTED

There seems to be a body of opinion that probably in retrospect it could have been handled a little more gracefully.
J. Carter Brown
Director emeritus, National Gallery of Art

Unlike most corporations that can hire and fire at will, museums must handle personnel issues in a manner that respects the professional dignity of the staff and the loyalties of supporters, while still achieving management objectives. Since museums operate in clear public view, they must always be prepared to respond effectively to controversy. We would suggest that all museums keep these principles in mind.
Andrew Camden
Charles Dambach
Chairman, and President and CEO, Museum Trustee Association

DUMBING DOWN

The downgrading of scholarship in museums is one of the most frightening trends at the moment, here in the [UK's] Department of Culture, Media, and Sport (DCMS), and, it now seems, in Boston.
Jennifer Montagu
The Warburg Institute, University of London

A serious, but fundamental, problem with American museums lies in the simple fact that museum staff are often more talented than the directors who supervise them. "Restructuring" is the best way to rid an organization of independent thinkers an insecure administration considers threatening.
Christina H. Nelson
European and American decorative arts, Nelson-Atkins Museum

Throwing African art in with Asian reveals only one possible guiding principle: you are creating a Department of Coloured Art, black and yellow together.
Madeline H. Caviness
Professor of Art History, Tufts University

Why not just eliminate them all [the departments] and save the money. Truly, the dumbing down of the MFA has arrived.
Dale Broholm
Furniture designer

ANTI-CURATORIAL

Usually, when such mega-departments are created the end result is that a layer of bureaucracy is added, and/or quality diminishes.
James Moore
Director, the Albuquerque Museum, New Mexico

We see this scheme as a political coup designed to enhance the director's role and diminish that of the curator, giving priority to development and marketing, while leaving the main work of the museum to inexperienced curators and temporary consultants who will report to area administrators.
Mr and Mrs H.A. Crosby Forbes
MFA patrons

To fire a curator of Jonathan [Fairbank's] experience and stature is [an] insult to the American museum profession.
Lewis Sharp
Director, Denver Art Museum

A very damaging assault on curatorial responsibility is afoot. The divorce of knowledge from responsibility was the worst aspect of the proposed Esteve-Coll restructuring of the V&A in 1989.
John Mallet
President, English Ceramic Circle

Curators who were hired to do a specific job now find themselves having to fulfil duties for which they are ill-equipped. All this needs to be scrutinized and explained to the community.
Fred Licht
Curator of the Peggy Guggenheim Collection, Venice

UNPROFESSIONAL

The procedure by which these dismissals were decided and effected flouts the long tradition of civility sustained by MFA and other distinguished art museums [and evinces] a disrespect for the values of scholarship and expertise.
Eight curators
Smithsonian National Museum of American History

In reorganising the collections and publicly humiliating long-standing curators, the director has angered professionals across the country. [The plan] appears to be thoroughly anti-intellectual, and disrespectful.
Wanda M. Corn
Historian of American art, Stanford University

The cost of violating professional standards is usually quite high: the alienation of donors, friends, colleagues of the persons fired, all of whom can legitimately feel in this instance that the right steps were not taken.
David D. Hall
Professor of American Religious History, Harvard Divinity School

When a distinguished institution demonstrates disregard for the dignity of its employees the well being of the entire profession is threatened.
DeCourcy McIntosh
Executive director, Frick Art & Historical Center, Pittsburgh

DAMAGING

You insulted the whole field of American material culture. You have become a pariah institution in the eyes of thousands of people who believe that American decorative arts are a significant field deserving of an expert curator.
Alfred C. Harrison
President of North Point Gallery, San Francisco, member Walpole Society, and grandson of Winterthur Museum founder Henry du Pont

As institutions of higher learning, [museums] should bear a certain responsibility to set an example, to address and conduct themselves according to the fine art of humanitarian principles. There has been nothing ennobling about this.
Elizabeth D. Garrett
Head of education, Christie's NY

ALIENATING

If the purpose was to create one museum it seems to be failing, because we have never seen the museum as seriously divided.
Kathleen D. and Clarence A. Kemper
MFA patrons

Why contribute art or money to an institution that treats its own employees, and perhaps the money and works of art those donors contribute, so cavalierly?
David Grayson Alles
Business historian, Concord, Mass

How are collectors and supporters to be assured that their wishes, collections, family heirlooms and heartfelt generosity are not to be so blatantly dismissed and used for generic purposes by a future administrator?
Stewart W. Thompso
President, Society of Arts and Crafts, Bosto

Compiled by **J.E.B**

Letters of protest, etc.,
printed in the Art Newspaper of September, 1999

Back at the Museum, most of the remaining curators naturally hated what had happened. Had they organized, all sympathy would have been with them. But the Museum management had done well to take away their leadership. No one made a peep. The newspapers clamored for comments from anyone who worked or had worked at the Museum, but couldn't find any. The only one who said anything to the papers was me. And our union consultant Paul McCarthy was pissed off about it. "This isn't your fight," he said, "Your people won't gain anything by your speaking out. Let them fight their own battles." They didn't. Some even stuck knives in the backs of others to gain the newly opened positions

One day after work, about two or three months later, I ran into Jonathan Fairbanks in the parking lot outside the Museum. He told me how he had gone back to his old haunts in the Southwest. He had been brought up in Utah. There he consulted some trusted friends among the Hopi elders, whom he very much admired. They gave him a lot of consolation and spiritual solace, and they strongly advised him not to get embroiled in any battles with the Museum. Perhaps it was best for him to really start clean and fresh, away from a museum where Jonathan had heard Malcolm Rogers describe curators as "changeable spokes in a wheel." Jonathan did just that, taking a job as director of the Fuller Craft Museum in Brockton, Massachusetts.

"Michael," he said to me, "The Hopi elders were very helpful and understanding. But they made it clear that in no way should I engage or have anything to do with the Museum." So, just like that, the end came for Jonathan Fairbanks of over thirty heartfelt years at an institution that he loved dearly and with people who were like family to him.

19

Wisdom, hereditary wisdom, verily
Is your proud boast; but at the haughty claim
The Mentors of the Mob are mocking merrily,--
And who is the blame?

--*Punch* 1884

THE PRE-CORPORATE MUSEUM

(Taking a long and realistic view of the ills in "Paradise")

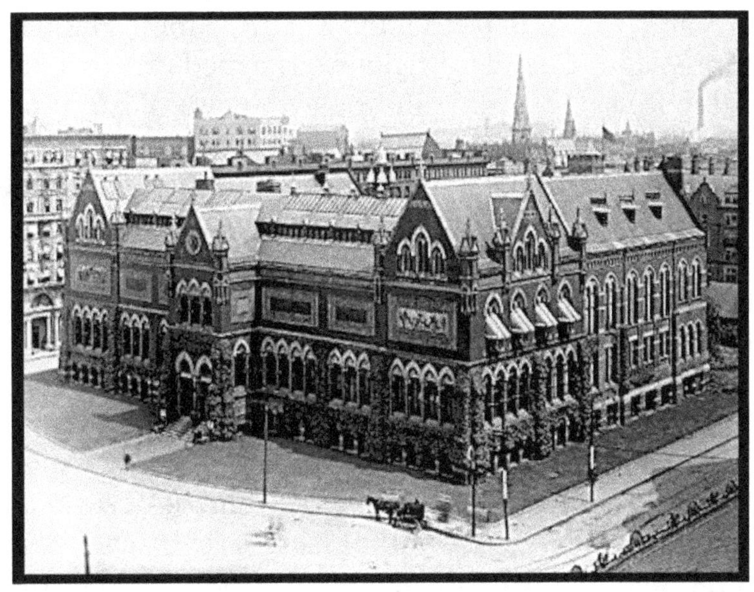

The original Building of the Boston Museum of Fine Arts in Copley Square, Boston. It was finished in 1876 and torn down in 1911. (Photograph from the Boston MFA archives)

I have said previously that the pre-corporate Museum was not ideal but that it seemed so. Quite possibly that was because I came at a time when guards were pretty much left alone in the galleries to do their job and enjoy the art. For me, it was like a farmer putting the cows out into the finest and most beautiful pasture they had ever seen or dreamed of, with the only admonition being, "Take good care of the calves." Well, the cows are not going to be very critical of the farmer's other habits.

The Museum was originally founded by Martin Brimmer and Charles C. Perkins, with Emil Otto Grundman as the first director. Brimmer was both a businessman and a successful politician who had attended Harvard University. Perkins was also a Harvard graduate and was independently wealthy. John Hubbard Sturgis and Charles Brigham designed the original Gothic Revival building in Copley Square, Boston, pictured above. Guy Lowell was the architect who created the present Museum building on Huntington Avenue, with additions finished in 2010 by Norman Foster.

As a matter of fact, the Boston Brahmins who created the Museum as their own club and opened it to the public were the previous monarchy in Boston. They controlled Boston for a century, until they were deposed. Like most millionaires of the time, they had obtained their ill-gotten gains on the blood and bodies of many others. As part of their empire, they made great mansions and filled them with assorted treasures. They didn't know much about these treasures, but they admired those who did, and they courted their approval. And as "philanthropists," they sought ways to share a little bit of their "culture" with the great masses. Thus, they established institutions such as the Museum and Symphony Hall.

First, there were the rapacious art dealers, who made big bucks off of the Brahmins. Then, the Brahmins gathered a coterie of the finest academics and scholars they could find to help run their institutions. They were less greedy for money—which they already had in abundance—than they were for approval and expiation.

The curators had their own class structure. After all, they had gone to the finest universities and spent years culling their knowledge from the great teachers there. In their mind, *they* were the aristocracy.

It's true that each department had its own secret compound in the Museum, hidden away from the public. There they did, well, what they did. There they stayed for the day, and I was always surprised that there was only one curator in the whole Museum who regularly availed himself of the opportunity to travel about the Museum and feast his eyes on the artworks of the other departments.

The system of teaching in the Museum was much like the system in all museums. The wives of the rich and influential husbands (read: donors) became docent ladies. They had absolutely no background in art, but they were trained in the prevailing views of the day for about one month. Then they set forth to teach, in turn, the masses of school children who came on field trips to the Museum. They would show them exhibit rooms of the stately houses of the rich which most of the children would never enter in real life, and so on. In this way the social structure and its ways were upheld. That is, it was not really experience and knowledge that mattered in the end, but riches and status.

Once, when I was at a small gathering, one of the men there wrote for a New England Art Journal. When he heard I worked at the Boston Museum of Fine Arts, he asked me, "What is the one thing in the Museum that you dislike the most. Without hesitating, I said, "Listening to the docent ladies." His wife and his mother-in-law were also there. The wife immediately began laughing. I asked why. Choking back her laughter, she pointed to her mother. "She's a docent lady!"

What can I say? Once I was in a gallery where two Dutch portraits stood side by side. One was mediocre. One was spectacular. A docent lady was there. I asked her, "Which one of these paintings do you think is the best?" She looked for a moment and picked the great one. I asked her why. She said honestly, "Because our docent teacher told us it was great."

Recently, we are learning that much of the great art in Museums was looted. I am sad to say that even some of my favorite curators were guilty of dealing with known looters. This was another integral part of the old-time Museums. It seems they all did it. The MFA is and has been the subject of a number of lawsuits in this area. Even my hero among curators, Cornelius Vermeule, has had his name besmirched by dealing with known crooks in order to get masterworks of classical Greek and Roman art for the Museum (See the chapter on Dr. Vermeule later in the book). Cornelius, much beloved over the world as he was, had the reputation of a swashbuckler in acquiring antique works for the Museum. (One of his chief contacts was the well-known looter, Robert Hecht, who worked out of Italy.)

The Brahmins who donated the art were equally culpable. My understanding is that only rarely were they scrupulous in how they acquired the artworks that they passed on to the Museum.

Dr. Vermeule dealt with Robert Hecht fairly extensively. Hecht was connected with the most famous case of looting, that of Marion True, an esteemed curator and scholar at the Getty Museum, along with Hecht's cohort Giacomo Medici. They were said to be involved in selling huge amounts of stolen art to the Getty (and many other institutions), including famous statues of Aphrodite and Apollo, along with many great vessels and urns. These were works of art of the highest merit and would bring any museum that got them to the top rank of Classical Art collections in the world. I believe that both the Italian and Greek governments were involved in prosecuting the case. It got banner headlines and really marked the end of an era, because, in reality, a number of the big Museums were deeply implicated in such trafficking.

The Boston Museum of Fine Arts as it is today on Huntington Avenue in Boston.

Not just the Boston Brahmins, but also most museums the world over have made their Museum in the image of the rich. All museumgoers know the work of the great Renaissance painters, and the great Baroque painters, etc. These were all done for rich patrons, or the richest of patrons, the church. Most of the Egyptian art is from the tombs of the Pharaohs and the rich and powerful Egyptians of the time. And so on. While those artworks are worth venerating, they are only a small percentage of the art that was done at any given time. Far more numerous was the art that was done by the "*people:*" folk art. There is a section in the Museum for the folk art of New England. But you will see little or nothing of the folk art of other places and other ages. And most other museums are the same. In this way, the museum visitor goes away with a very stilted view of art in its totality.

Such was the old-time Museum in Boston, and, in fact, old-time Museums all over the world. To the corporate giants, they must have looked archaic, antiquated and easy pickings. I suppose you could say we went from the art of the rich or art through the eyes of the rich to the art of valuable commodities through the eyes of those who became rich by buying and selling valuable commodities (or advising others how to do so).

Eleanor Sayers was the granddaughter of Woodrow Wilson. She was a respected curator of the old Boston Museum, considered one of the great scholars of the life and work of the artist, Francisco Goya. Her retirement from the Museum came soon after the Boston Massacre. There was a farewell assembly for her in the Museum auditorium. I remember vividly watching an ancient trustee from the old days climbing up the stairs to give a testimonial. He was stooped, gaunt, with a cane. He barely made it. It was an apt picture of the end of the Brahmin reign.

20

If your master is surly from getting up early
(And tempers are short in the morning),
An inopportune joke is enough to provoke
Him to give you, at once, a month's warning.

--from The Yeomen of the Guard
by Gilbert and Sullivan

A CAUTIONARY TALE

Perhaps the most sinister and offensive figure in all my days at the Museum was John Paul Kozicki. He came from La-La Land, which, for him, was head concierge at The Motion Picture Museum in New York. He arrived in 1998, just before the Boston Massacre, and, with my nose for plots by management real and imaginary, I'm surprised I never considered that coincidence to be premeditated, until now.

Kozicki was the new head of Visitor Services, which itself was a new department, and suddenly we came under its umbrella. He exuded "I'm nice." "I'm idealistic." "I want to help you." "Come into my office whenever you want." In point of fact, he was mean and uncaring—and he would probably cry if he heard me say that. In all the time he was at the Museum, I cannot remember even one grievance that he accepted at his stage of the process. I cannot remember one time that he agreed with the union's position on anything.

When I did come into his office, he would talk as if he was taking me into his confidence, and I was surprised at the things he would tell me. He would reveal all sorts of things about his life—things that I didn't want to know. Then he would talk about his ideals and his wonderful plans. I would hear about all the great things that the new Visitor Services Department was going to do for the Museum and for the security guards. And he would act as if he was really interested in me and what I had to say. But by the time I left, he had invariably rejected everything I said. He seemed as if he liked you but he didn't. Under his watch, the "Team Leaders" came into being. They were semi-supervisors who began to patrol the floors of the Museum. They did cover for bathroom breaks—but if you called for one, they could be an hour in coming. Other than that, it was just another small group of people who could—and would—get you written up for some offense.

After the Massacre in 1999, we had our second contract campaign as an independent. It was long, very long, and management would not give an inch. Of course, we did our demonstrations, but at length, our guys just tired out. We were dead in the water. Which was just what management wanted. In their minds we were ripe for the picking. I thought about it. I was damned if I was going to let the Museum wear us down. I came up with a plan. Only the treasurer and myself were in on it.

Gary Lombard, one of our best union guys, had left the Museum. Over the years, Gary had been involved in many wild and daring adventures in pursuit of, well, fighting management. You will hear even more about that elsewhere in the book.

Gary was trying to get his own business going as a computer techie, but it was not easy. So I called and got him to work for us five days a week. Every day, he put up our 25-foot and 30-foot signs. He stapled leaflets on every tree around the Museum and put them on every car, too. Plus, he handed out leaflets to cars and people coming in to the Museum. Five days out of seven, Gary was out there. On the weekends, a few others and myself came out. Someone was always there.

After a while, Gary complained, "It's getting lonely out there all by myself. I need some company!" So Jim Kowalski, the treasurer and I hired another ex-guard, Jim Manning, also starting out as an art entrepreneur, to work with Gary twice a week. Jim is currently working as an independent curator, artist, and film producer in the Boston area. Anyway, the strategy worked. We wore the Museum down, instead of them wearing us down.

Gary Lombard picketing in front of the Museum

Once again, we were alive and well. Not so, John Paul. Our union victory was on his watch, and the Museum management took it personally. He was fired soon after. He cried.

After Kozicki was fired, Jim Beneway took over and Security was once again Security. Jim had been both a guard and then a longtime supervisor. He was almost universally disliked by the guards. Some of them nicknamed him "Rambo."

Jim did not have a warm and fuzzy exterior. But I could work out grievances and other problems with him. He actually cared a lot for the guards. After all, he had been one. If I appealed to that side of Jim, he almost always responded–unless he had gotten his marching orders from above. I would relate to him as someone who I knew to be a good person, someone I could expect to do the right thing. I would say, "Jim, this guy needs your help. He is going through a lot of health problems and if he loses his job, it would be catastrophic for him." He did listen and he did care. For certain people, he would go way beyond the call of duty. And generally I was the only one who knew he did it.

I enjoyed working with Jim Beneway. As director of Security–or more properly, Protective Services, in the new Museum terminology– he actually lasted through two contract campaigns with us, 2002 and 2005–6, before he was fired. I don't know how he did it, but he was the only head of Security to do so.

21

Don't ask about my principles, they're flexible as hell
I'm a modern politician, I represent you well.
--from The Candidate and The Elector
by Smokey Dymny

THE DEMOCRATIC NATIONAL CONVENTION

In 2004, the Democratic Party held its convention in Boston, when our union was not facing another contract negotiation fight. My wife remembers coming home from the convention in which John Kerry was nominated for president. She told me, "I have just heard the first black man who will become president of the United States." Nowadays, she adds, "But I didn't think it would be so quick." My wife had heard Barack Obama, who gave the nominating speech for Kerry.

This was the period just leading up to contract negotiation, but not yet that time. My feeling was, never let a good opportunity pass you by, and this was an excellent opportunity to get our engine running and our guys into the mix. Of course, it represented a great audience and a chance to put the Museum on the defensive.

The first day was the party of the rank and file, the delegates to the convention. These were the common people, workers like us; lots of teachers, too, I remember. These people were sympathetic and encouraging. They wished us well and talked to us about our problems. They took our leaflets and promised to communicate their concerns to the Museum management.

The following day was the party of the bigwigs: the donors, the swells and the fundraisers. As much as the delegates were encouraging, the bigwigs were

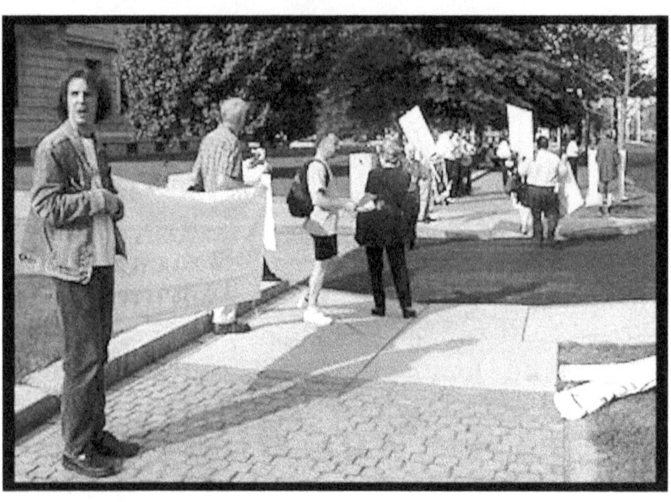

MISU members picketing outside the Museum during one of the DNC parties.

disapproving, aloof and unfriendly. I guess they felt we were raining on their parade. I remember there was one well fed and well-suited Democratic official going into the party, passing by us leafleteers. I tried to get him to take a leaflet and he rather pompously and haughtily waved me off. I said to him, “Don’t you know that *we are your constituency?*” He gave me a derisive look. “You guys are acting just like Republicans!” I yelled. He kind of smiled and for a second, I think he got it. And then he walked on. Without taking the leaflet!

It never occurred to me at the time that the leaflets we handed out, describing how the Museum treated their workers, might also describe how these high-brow delegates treated *their* employees. Nor did it strike my mind that the signs and pickets we held could have been taken very personally by some of these guys — and it was mainly *guys* — that we could have been their workers, having the exact same complaints.

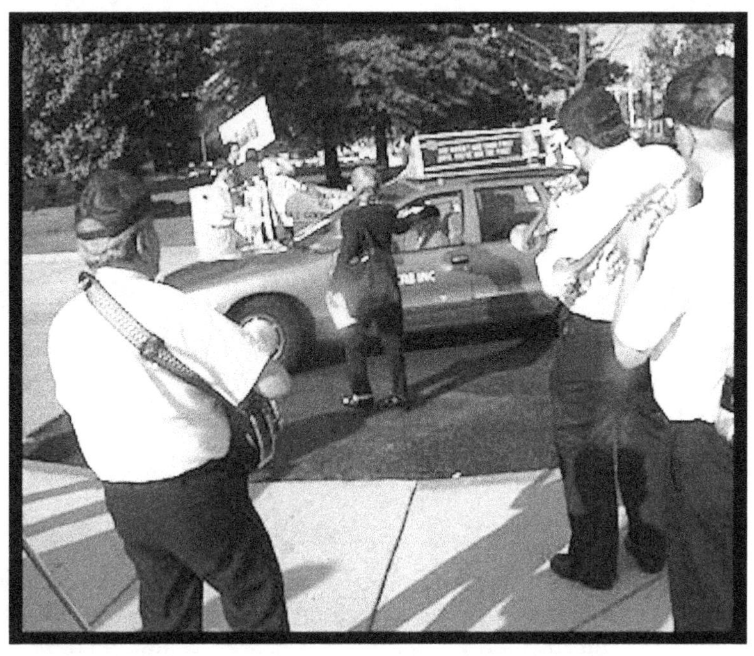

Our wonderful Union Band outside the Museum, at a DNC party, playing for an incoming partygoer.

Later in the week it was the night for Hillary, Bill, Teddy and the like. A representative from the Massachusetts AFL-CIO called us and said that if we wanted, they would not cross the picket line and that they would even cancel the whole thing. We told them, "No, it was all right, they should go ahead." The truth was that we weren't planning anything for that night. While we did know that the big guns were going to be there, we also knew that it was just a very small party. So we decided to rest our people that night.

In a nutshell, those three nights epitomize the problem of our political system. At least, that's what I took away. It was eye opening for me. I will not forget the fat cats of that second night. Naïve as I was, I didn't expect

An unidentified union member with a cartoon based on a pair of Museum paintings of George and Martha Washington by Gilbert Stuart. Martha says to George, "I hear the MFA is making a $425 million expansion, Georgie." And George replies, "Yes dear, they are building another empire at our expense!"

that Democrats would deride the efforts of a labor union exercising their rights. The problem was not with the people, the rank and file. The problem wasn't even with the candidates, flawed as they might be.

Alas, the problem was that the same corporate takeover that I have described at the Museum had happened with both the Republicans and the Democrats. If these corporate leaders of the party treated their workers badly, as I believe many or most of them did and do, how could we expect them to work to help us in our problems? How could we expect them to want to better our working conditions? What we can expect them to do is exactly what they are doi

22

Let America be the dream that Dreamers dreamed
Let it be that great strong land of love.

from *Let America Be America Again*
by Langston Hughes

OUR POLITICIANS

Ultimately you must reach out to the community beyond. It is like finding your greater self.

2005 and 2006 were my last years at the Museum before I retired. These were also the years of the final contract campaign of my career as a worker at the Boston MFA. Indeed, it was a marathon and a monumental campaign lasting a year or more, starting in the spring of 2005 and lasting into the summer of 2006.

The connection with our local politicians started one day when I went with my wife to a talk by an African American state representative from Boston's South End, Byron Rushing, at a church in Roxbury. Muriel (my wife) had had extensive dealings with Byron in her work as an immigrant rights advocate. She called him "the saint."

Listening, I became aware of Byron's more than considerable knowledge and interest in the history of Roxbury and its importance to the African American heritage. He had served as president of the Museum of Afro-American History from 1972 to 1985.

I also noted Byron's deep concern that institutions like the Museum of Fine Arts, even though they were located in the very midst of that area of Boston, had exhibited a total disregard of that heritage.

It must be noted that Roxbury is home to where a great part of Boston's African American history took place and where those who made it lived. And it is largely ignored. Depending on how you look at it, the Boston Museum of Fine Arts is either on the edge of that area, or at its center. Byron Rushing saw it as at the very center.

To be fair, the Museum did have one Black curator, Barry Gaithers, although he wasn't even part of the Museum proper. He worked at a small satellite building elsewhere in Roxbury. If you didn't know about it, the Museum generally didn't tell you. Almost all African American material from and about Roxbury was shunted there.

I came away from his talk with the impression that it was of intense personal importance to him to challenge and change that indifference.

There was almost no minority presence of color on the Museum staff except for the cleaners and us. We guards however were like a United Nations of the world, just what the staff of an institution with world-class art from all cultures of the earth should be. All colors, all ethnicities, all nationalities and all types. And because we had a union, we wielded considerable power.

I came away from the talk with another thought: that Byron and the security guard union of the MFA had strong mutual interests, though we were coming at it from very different angles. Certainly, we both had strong issues with the Museum. Perhaps we could help each other.

With the aid of my wife, I was able to get a meeting with Byron, and he was indeed interested. Byron, in fact, went far beyond any of my expectations, saying, "Let us

The author meeting with Byron Rushing for the first time in his office.

see who else we can get involved." He went on to set up a connection with all the politicians in the Roxbury area: Chuck Turner, Felix Arroyo, Diane Wilkerson and Gloria Fox. They were all minorities. They all liked the idea. Ultimately, they all agreed to work with us.

I remember that when I went to see Felix Arroyo, I ran into Rand Wilson. He was several incarnations away from being the head of Jobs With Justice. At this time, he was working with SEIU, the Service Workers' Union. "What are you doing here?" I asked Rand. "Same thing as you," he replied, "Begging."

The minority politicians of the Roxbury area formed a strategic auxiliary force. When needed, they could inflict embarrassment and punishment. If the Corporate Museum had a conscience, these politicians, by their very makeup, stood for much that was morally missing from the Museum. If a conscience was not there, they were a reminder of that emptiness at the heart of the

Felix Arroyo with the author

Museum. They had a power and credibility that the Museum lacked. I also found them, for the most part, to be wonderful people to work with, especially Byron and Chuck Turner, who left me with many fond remembrances of what real politicians could be like.

Most of the time, the politicians were more or less in the background. It was in the endgame of the union contract negotiation campaign, when the Museum management was refusing to budge, that our political allies came to the forefront. Then they even went unbidden to a meeting of the Board of Trustees to support our efforts. I really don't know what actually happened. I can only attempt to envision these five politicians, black and Latino, walking in on the all-white body of corporate bigwigs and stuffed shirts. That was the first strike.

The second strike came a few days later when Felix, Byron and Chuck all gave excellent speeches at the last rally of the campaign, the one just before the Museum capitulated.

With Chuck Turner

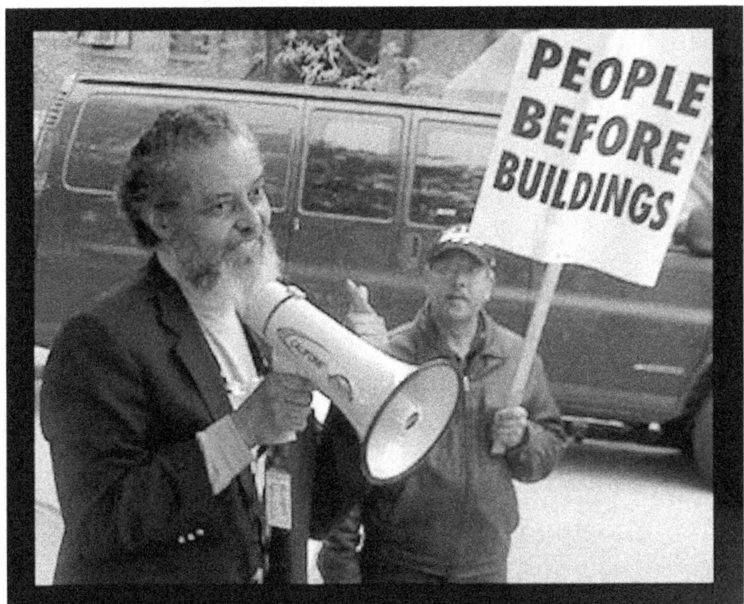

Byron with MISU's Carlos Oviedo

Carlos Oviedo, Mary Berry, Gloria Fox, The author, and Marilyn Leung

Afterwards, I got together with the politicians in a victory celebration meeting. We took pictures and all that. But now it was their turn. They wanted us to help them organize the security guards of Northeastern University, a nearby institution also on the border of Roxbury. I said I would look forward to that.

In order to get this process going, I needed to get the approval of our Union Executive Board. Despite all of my efforts to persuade them to approve the idea, I came up empty. "Are you going to make me go back having to explain this, after they came through for us?" "Sorry, Michael, we have neither the funds nor the inclination." Only one person on the Board voted with me in my motion to help organize Northeastern. Alas, it was one of my biggest disappointments.

There is a great lesson here! Though I thought the board's decision was wrong, I realized later it would have been a big mistake to stretch our resources thin in working to organize the Northeastern guards. The lesson was to let go of my ego, and accept what my brothers and sisters on the Executive Board saw as the more realistic decision.

Nevertheless, we owe deepest appreciation to the politicians who were essential in our victory.

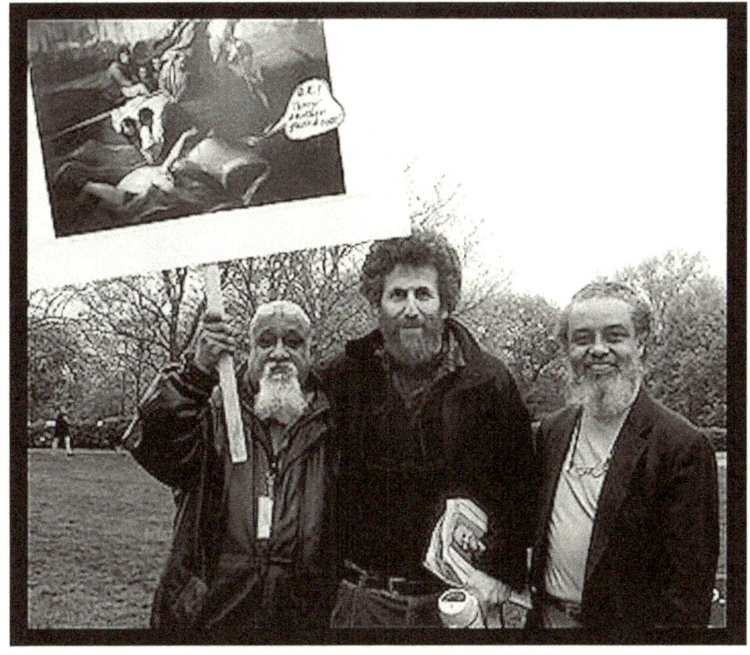

With Chuck Turner and Byron Rushing. The cartoon Chuck is holding up is from the famous painting of Watson and the Shark by John Singleton Copley. The shark is saying, "O.K.! Throw another guard over!"

Oh how the workers yelled
Oh how we hugged and cried
Oh how we loved this day.
--from *Waving on the Breeze* by Jim Sharp

A TYPICAL DEMONSTRATION

Let me describe a typical demonstration. We had been agitating and leafleting on a contract campaign from 2005 to 2006. It was a campaign in which we had yet to win any of our issues. Management is hoping we will tire out and die. They're licking their chops at that thought. Paul McCarthy, our main labor consultantri Pa, is faulting me for not pushing hard enough. We are in desperate need of an outrageous demonstration to rock management's boat. That type of "Typical Demonstration" is what I am talking about.

At this time Lisa Rhea was working the front desk, checking people in and out of the innards of the Museum. She also had the monthly event calendar of the Museum at her side. So we asked her, "Lisa, what are the most important parties for the coming month?" We went down the list. All of a sudden, "Ah! There it is!" Lisa pointed out the Big One: the one where the most important people will come. The one where the Museum is looking to make the best impression. The one where we can embarrass them the most. "O.K. We have identified the event!"

The event was to be the party honoring Bill Koch, the multi-billionaire. The backdrop is that Koch had been on the MFA's board and had quit. Now he was back and the Museum was exhibiting his collection of paintings.

He was dangling them temptingly before them in a way to make them hope he would ultimately donate them to the Boston MFA. Of course, he made no promises. His position was deliberately ambiguous. In front of the Museum, on the lawn were two of Koch's racing yachts. Have I mentioned that he and his crew had won the prized America's Cup with one of them, America 3 or *America Cubed?* And have I mentioned that he was a "Koch brother"? Actually the third Koch brother.

The famous Koch brothers consist of his twin brother and his older brother. There had been a long war between the siblings over control of Koch Industries. Arch conservatism and money run in the family. The father, who is said to be one of the founders of the John Birch Society, also founded Koch Industries. Bill himself is said to be worth 4 billion dollars. He had taken his company, the Oxbow Group or Oxbow Carbon, whose main product is calcined petroleum coke, out of Massachusetts in order to pay lower taxes in Florida. He also formed the Oxbow lobby against the Cape Wind project off Nantucket. He contributed close to a billion dollars to the presidential campaign of Mitt Romney. (More recently, in the present time frame, he was also a huge contributor to Donald Trump's campaign. And that includes hosting a $50,000 a head fund raising dinner for him.)

So the Museum was going all-out to woo him back into the fold and he was playing coy. This party was a gala event to impress him—just such an event to give us the maximum bang for our buck![3] It couldn't have been better. Our mouths watered.

Did I mention that Koch, like his brothers, was rabidly anti-union?

After this discovery, I called a meeting of the executive board, not an easy group to get together on short notice given all the different schedules they were on. I needed to argue for the necessity of the huge demonstration I envisioned, and to get all the executive board members on board for such an undertaking. Actually, I do not remember encountering any opposition after I explained it to them. They also became excited. Russell Gilfoy, who came from both a drama and visual arts background, saw this as just his cup of tea. He immediately volunteered to help with the signs and other artistic enterprises.

Not to be outdone, John Storrow yelled, “ME, too!” He would make up pirate flags to go along with Koch’s boats. John actually came from a boating tradition and had made several boats by himself, both regular and models, besides making numerous fanciful paintings of boats and ships.

It was not lost on us that the skull and crossbones on pirate flags are known as the “Jolly Roger”, as we so dubbed the Pirate Malcolm Rogers for that night.

We thought up new ideas for signs and leaflets, which we would make at the local “Red Sun” printers, an employee owned union shop. We came up with ideas like “Don’t Let the Museum Sink our Ship,” “We Need To Stay Afloat,” etc. Some of the slogans and art ideas came from John Storrow’s wife, Lisa Graf.

Of course, we would engage our union band; everyone was in favor of that, as they were of inviting our politicians and having them speak, if possible. Jim Kowalski and Carlos Oviedo, our “old dependables” and also Union Executive Board members, would be responsible for getting all our signs, banners and other paraphernalia in front of the Museum in a timely way. I would bring the leaflets and act as contact man for all the outside groups we worked with.

DON'T SINK OUR BOAT!

WE NEED TO STAY AFLOAT!

We, the low-wage Security Guards of the MFA are fighting for our economic lives. In over half a year of negotiations, the Museum has refused to back off their demands for drastic cuts in our already small wages. The same Museum had an excellent year in 2004 with huge profits all across the board. It began an ambitious $525 million building expansion. Their director, Malcolm Rogers, made $567,00, including a $55,000 raise in pay and benefits.

- **So why in the age of post 9/11 did he cut 10% of his security guard force?**
- **Why does he want to take money away from his frontline low-wage workers?**
- **Why won't he negotiate with his low-wage security guards in good faith?**
- **And why does he cry poor?**

We are fighting for fairness. If you love and care for the Museum, please help the people who work there. Please e-mail letters of support to mfaguards@hotmail.com or write to *MFA Guards, P.O. Box 230815 Astor Station, Boston MA 02123.*

Our flyer: "Don't Sink Our Boat!"

Everything had to be at its height. I had to get, if possible, every group that had worked with us to come. These included Jobs with Justice, the Carpenters' Union the Teamsters, GALLAN (the gay rights group), Billionaires for Bush (a great street theater group), United For a Fair Economy, SLAP (the college activists), MALC (Massachusetts Artists Leaders Coalition), art students from the Museum School and MassArt, and more I may have forgotten.

We needed our politicians to come out, and, hopefully, a large crowd would encourage them to give a speech. We needed our band. And, most of all, we needed our own people to come out.

The main thing was to have all our people and supporters invited and involved, understanding the immensity of the event, a kind of “Can’t Miss” on their social calendar. So we sent out calls and e-mails emphasizing the notorious Koch and his famous boats in front of the Boston Museum of Fine Arts, adding to that: prominent politicians, a marching band and street theater. And, of course, the high stakes that were involved for our labor union.

Then we went around telling our own people how important this was. But there are always union members who say they will be out there and who have no intention of actually coming. But here a few influential people got the message loud and clear.

Foremost among them was Brenda Lee, the longest serving gallery guard at the MFA with a lot of clout when she wanted to use it. Brenda worked plenty of overtime and knew all the others who regularly worked overtime. Let us say she exerted a lot of pressure on those people. Brenda, practically single

Brenda Lee

handed did the impossible by convincing almost all the guards to forego overtime and join in the Koch demonstration "You best not be working that night, if you know what's good for you!" And then the totally unheard of happened: almost all the guards declined the overtime work of that party.

Finally, we contacted the pols. Would they come out? We described the situation. We said that crowds would come. It appealed to them. They would be there.

Then, as a wild card, I began to write an Op-Ed piece for the Boston Globe. I asked my wife about that. "Do you know how hard it is to get the Globe to accept an Op-Ed piece? You'll never do it," said she. But she gave me the name of a woman she knew who worked on their editorial board. "Thanks," I said, "Let's see what happens." And I continued writing. (I also got a few tips from that woman on the editorial board.) Less than a week before the demonstration, I sent the piece off, confident they wouldn't use it.

24

Banners blazing bright, hoist them high, hoist them high
We are marching to the beating of an everlasting drum.
--from *The Everlasting Drum* by Jez Lowe

A TYPICAL DEMONSTRATION II

After work on the day of the big demonstration, I came out to set things up. Our main men, Carlos and Jim were there. They had all our signs and banners stowed in the back of their cars. Jim and I discussed the weather. Carlos guessed at how many people would come. It would be a couple of hours before the party started. A few other people were there also to help put things together. But the turnout seemed pretty sparse at that point, though the weather was perfect.

Koch's boats made a fine backdrop for all of our stuff. By surprise, someone came by with the Giant Rat, which was a kind of mascot of the Teamster's Union. It seemed as if things might be working for us. Someone put "Malcolm Rogers" around its neck. Someone else added his huge salary.

The hours before a demonstration were always the most nerve-wracking time. You never knew if anyone would really show up. You could be standing out there by yourself. Little by little, people did start showing up, our own and others. We put them to work. Storrow and Gilfoy came with their stuff. More and more people arrived. And then, more. At first, I sighed with relief. Then I sang with happiness. By the time the party began, there was a throng. Inside, the docent ladies were doing the work of the guards, all of whom were outside at the demonstration.

Bright and Sunny,
The Day of the Demonstration Comes

Four views of the "throngs" that came
to the Koch Demonstration

PEOPLE
BEFORE

We had our people with the most finesse stand at the entrance to the driveway where people were being dropped off for the party. So when the partygoers showed up in their cars, our folks looked and acted like greeters. I remember Jennifer Doe of Jobs With Justice being great at this. So was my wife. Politely, they stopped the cars and handed out our leaflets as if it were part of the show. "Welcome to the Museum. May we help you, sir/madam. Please take this and read it. Thank you. Have a good time at the party."

The band played and the politicians, Chuck Turner, Felix Arroyo and Byron Rushing all came and gave excellent speeches. Byron's talk, in particular, was an absolute classic. An extract is given, below, and a transcription of the whole talk can be seen in the appendix.

Byron Rushing giving his talk

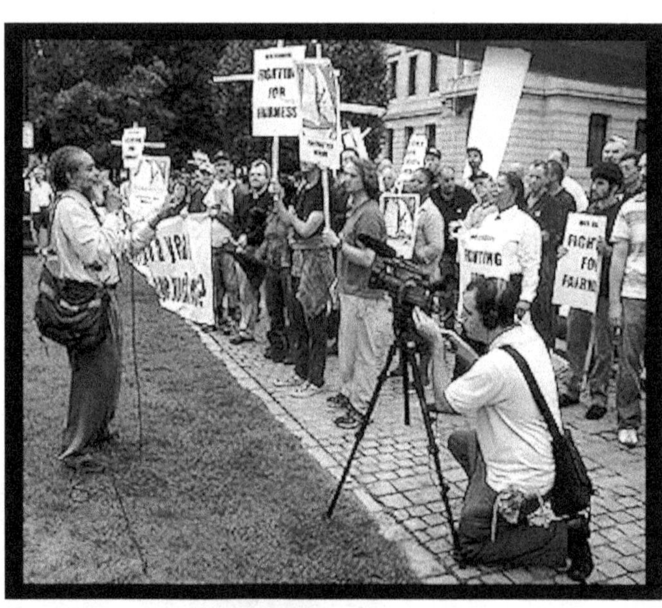

A short extract from Byron Rushing's talk at the Koch Demonstration: *"This MFA is a world class disgrace when it comes to major art museums. The community around the museum is in the same relationship to this museum that Harlem was to the Metropolitan at the end of the 1960s. We are in that kind of situation. And what you are doing is just part of what all community people should be doing, and that is telling the truth about what is really going on at the MFA."*

Our songs and chants echoed off the walls of the Museum. A new banner, thirty feet in length, made for us by the carpenters' union, fluttered in the breeze. Pirate flags waved and the party goers came out to the doorway to see what was happening with mouths agape. Chuck Turner actually went up to and inside the Museum handing out leaflets to the partiers, until he was finally kicked out. Billionaires for Bush put on some very humorous street theater. The whole thing was a grand show.

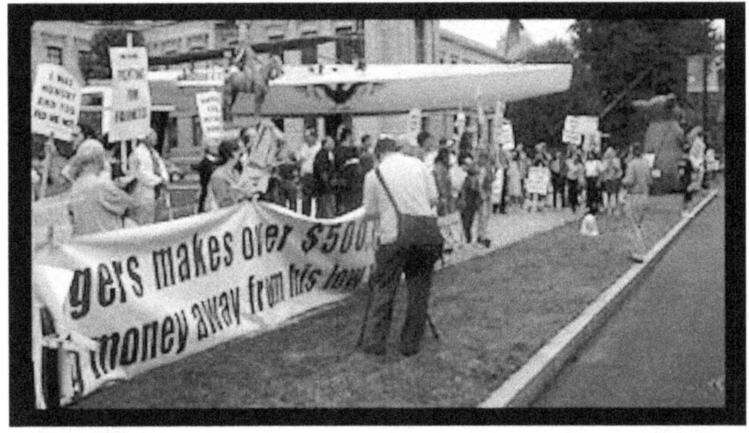

A last view of the demonstration, with Koch's winning yacht, (dubbed by us the "S.S. Jolly Roger"). If you look carefully, you can see the Giant Rat in the far right hand corner

And, oh yes, the next day, the Op-Ed piece was printed front and center in the Boston Globe.

Two days later, the Museum management finally capitulated on the issues that we needed, including keeping all benefits intact and a healthy pay raise. We had a contract!

URSDAY, SEPTEMBER 1, 2005 THE BOSTON GLOBE Opinion A19

MICHAEL RAYSSON

The new corporate MFA

ACING THE front lawn of Boston's seum of Fine Arts are two huge and amlined American Cup yachts with foot masts. They are a fitting introduc- n to the *new* MFA, which features the ts and art of multimillionaire Bill ch, the automobiles of fashion king ph Lauren, lavish parties for wealthy nors, and the half billion dollar expan- n of the museum that is to come.

Along with most other large art in- tutions in this country, the MFA has ne the way of profits, expansions, and pularity. Publicists, developers, and althy patrons rule at the top of the seum hierarchy. In all but tax status, e museum has become part of corporate erica, building wealth by whittling ay the salaries and benefits of its low- ge workers.

Having embraced corporate culture, e museum has also taken on some of its st characteristics. This has become pecially evident in the workplace. While seum director Malcolm Rogers and his lleagues in management make huge salaries with large raises, the rest of the museum staff has faced layoffs and cuts in salaries and/or benefits. Scholar curators have found themselves to be expendable pieces of the machine. Many staff members have gone years without a raise. The museum's low-wage security guards are now fighting for their life in contract negotiations.

The present standoff between the museum and their security guards has lasted half a year. These same guards serve at the museum's high-end parties and watch over their expensive treasures. They barely get by from week to week on what the MFA pays. According to salary.com, which compares all the security guards in the Boston area, they are in the lower 25th percentile for pay of all guards in Boston. By most standards, the MFA guards' annual income places them among the "working poor."

Yet Rogers claims they are highly paid. He has stood firm on *taking away* huge hunks of their wages and benefits even as he sees another banner year for the museum with the cash registers clinking far above expectations for the year.

The MFA's sizable profits in 2004 are detailed in museum board minutes of September 2004, telling of large MFA gains all across the board with their total assets increasing by almost $90 million dollars. Yet the museum had deliberately misled its own workers into believing that the MFA had hit upon hard times. Meanwhile, Rogers enjoyed a $55,000 raise to his $512,000 salary, while insisting that the layoffs were a "painful last resort" and salary cuts were part of "tough economic times."

Building its wealth by whittling away the salaries and benefits of its low-wage workers.

Because Rogers has cut 40 percent of the full-time gallery guard force since he came to the MFA, a majority of these guards are now part-time. Since they can't work 40 regular hours, they have to work overtime to make ends meet. But Rogers wants to cut any overtime pay except that over 40 hours (and that only because he has to pay it by law). This will cost many of these guards thousands of dollars. Not much money for Rogers, but for people who live from week to week, it's huge.

These scenarios come right out of the corporate notebook. But the public, which troops into the museum in ever-increasing numbers, still expects something different from an institution dedicated to the higher ideals of humanity. Indeed, state Senator Dianne Wilkerson, state Representatives Byron Rushing and Gloria Fox, and City Councilors Felix Arroyo and Chuck Turner, five community leaders who represent the area of the museum, came to see Rogers. They told him to get the takeaways off the table. They reminded him that the cuts from the guards' salaries would just about equal the raise in his salary. They told him that taking money away from his low-wage workers was not bargaining in good faith. Rogers, standing firm in his corporate ideals, ignored them.

Those leaders see in the security guards of the MFA the only department in the museum which represents the multicultural mix of their neighborhoods. The people who come to the museum from all over the world also see that mix. It reflects their own diversity and gives them a chance to ask questions of someone who understands their own language. Likewise, many guards have backgrounds which allow them to speak knowledgeably about the art in the museum. The guards take pride in their work and are happy to be the frontline ambassadors of the MFA. They should not be treated with *economic* contempt.

The sad thing is that we have to be talking about things like this. It should never happen in an institution like the MFA. The museum should be setting examples for corporations like Wal-mart, instead of taking lessons from them.

Michael Raysson *is president of the Museum Independent Security Union at Boston Museum of Fine Arts.*

The Op-Ed piece as it appeared in the Boston Globe

25

Is there aught we hold in common with the greedy parasite
Who would lash us into serfdom and would crush us with his might?
Is there anything left to us but to organize and fight?
For the union makes us strong

--*Solidarity Forever* by Ralph Chaplin

NEGOTIATIONS

Reality for most unions, and we were no exception, is that you have just so many issues or points on your agenda that you could expect management to accept in the end. Again and again Paul McCarthy would drum this home to me. "Prioritize. Find out what your people really want. Don't expend your capital on things that are relatively unimportant to them. Management will be happy to give them to you. Then, when the big things come, like a good pay raise, they will say, hey, we already gave you this that and the other." Usually, this comes down to two (or three at most) things that you will be willing to fight to the end for.

That admonition was extremely important. I would say it was the basis of all other negotiating strategy. For instance, it became clear to me that vacations, which were a big thing in my book, were of little importance to most of my fellow workers. Overtime was much more significant in their lives. Almost everybody was having trouble paying their bills, so the time-and-a-half was critical to their family's survival.

When I would go around talking to people individually to find out what the other guards wanted, no one ever said, “Vacations”. I might even ply them with, “Wouldn’t you like more vacation time?” If I even got a response, it was, “No, not really.”

Security Blanket

a publication of the Museum Independent Security Union
January 1999

What do We Want?

Important issues of the new contract negotiations
A letter from Michael Rayson

In Just a few weeks we will begin contract negotiations in earnest. We will present our proposals to the Museum and they will present their counter proposals.

What do we want? Malcolm Rodgers has said that it is the goal to have a staff that is "Highly motivated and highly rewarded" John Stanley has stated that he wants salaries that is competitive with those in the "outside world"

We agree and are taking those statements seriously. John Paul Kozicki, the head of Visitor Services recently visited the Museum of Modern Art in New York and having seen that museum stated that he appreciated what a good job we do. So we only want fair compensation and monetary appreciation for the job we do.

Recently a Study came out showing that we live in one of the most expensive cities in the nation. Our wages must reflect the extravagant cost of living in our city. The museum has just finished its most successful capital campaign in its history raising nearly $140 Million. The museum has also just finished its most successful show in its history which has apparently made a clear profit of seven million dollars. No bonus, not even a thank you was given. Some of the prosperity must be shared. We only want what is fair.

Some of our part time workers have no sick or vacation days. We are not in the middle ages. This must be changed and our members must be treated with respect and dignity and this includes fair wages and benefits. Management is about to adopt a new system using "Team Leaders" or "Lead Guards" Most of us in the union are not happy with this, bottom line is that more work is expected of us and there must be fair compensation.

Amongst night guards many conditions have not changed in ages and must be updated to be current with modern times.

All of the above (and more) must be taken in to account. We do not want to break the bank but we want what is fair. We will accept no less.Our wish is to work with the museum as a part of a happy family, but the museum on its part, can no longer act like a poor home. They must take care of its own.

What Bonus? by Michael Rayson

Having just finished the most successful show in the history of the museum. Congratulations are in order. Over 550,000 people visited and over seven million dollars clear profit was made. Right on the front lines were the security guards who had plenty to be proud of. So certainly when the it was all over and the profits counted up management might share just a little of those millions of dollars. Wrong! Not one penny of a bonus

I personally would like to appreciate all those who came in early every day and worked the long lines, all those who answered the questions, directed visitors and all those who dealt with masses at the doors and all those who showed visitors where <u>That Painting</u> was and so on. "Thanks" and so much more. There is an unfortunate lesson that left on its own, management will not do the right thing for the "museum family." Sometimes they have to be pushed to take care of those of us working on the front lines. Let us remember this with the negotiations at hand.

The other part of negotiations is that management also has their agenda, things that are important to them. In order to get a few things that you want, you may have to agree to a few things that they want. Neither side will be able to get everything they want.

Power is the name of the game. The Museum, of course, was one of the most powerful cultural institutions in Boston. We were just a small independent union with 120 low-wage workers. McCarthy would emphasize that we had little or no power *inside* the bargaining room. Since the Museum had all the power there, who could blame them for being bullies?

But outside, in the streets, it was another story. We could, and did, embarrass the Museum immensely. And how? Just by telling the truth. If they were spending half a billion dollars for building expansion, and then wouldn't give a piddling raise to their low-wage workers, now, how does that sound to the public?[3] It always amazed me that an institution dedicated to such high cultural standards could be so venal at heart. The only problem for us was how to tell this story in the most concise and yet expressive way possible.

At this time, management was making life miserable for guards with families, and was looking to implement rules in the contract to make their life even worse. When asked what guards in that position should do, the Museum lawyer answered, "Quit!" We quickly made up leaflets with pictures of guards and their children, illustrating this problem to the public and telling them to express themselves to museum management on how they felt about such draconian policies. After I handed one of these out to a museum patron, a mother with her children, I heard her say to them, "Dears, this is how the

Museum treats their family people!" It was music to my ears. Next bargaining meeting, management made huge concessions on this issue.

So the real skill in negotiating is not in making great arguments to management inside the bargaining room, it is in keeping the union members energized over the long haul of the campaign. It is in communicating with them so that morale remains high, even when management is trying to suck the air out of your sails. Making them feel that they are the most vital part of the process. That is most important. Second in importance is working magic out on the streets. Third, and only third, is surviving the deadly airs of the bargaining room and letting the first two steps work for you.

We tried to make our negotiating teams as representative as possible of the different segments of the bargaining unit. That was helpful in communicating to the members. It was helpful in gauging where we were at in any given time. And that was helpful in telling us how far we could go before it was time to stop and make an agreement that was in consonance with the general mood of our fellow workers. There is always one or two union member, and in our union it was usually me, who wants to push management as far as possible while the others are saying, "Enough is enough!" When the majority is exhausted, it is usually better to stop.

So far, I have only hinted at what things were like inside the negotiating room. I guess one does not like to relive anguish and torture. Even now, when I have had long experience, it is hard to convey the reality of sitting long, long hours across from management in those dismal rooms. However, lest someone accuse me of being remiss in conveying all aspects of union organizing, I will describe the experience as best I can.

No matter how long I was negotiating, I still went in with full optimism and high spirits. And always, like some mythical demonic and magical beast, management would draw the life out of us and our hopes and I would realize that we had missed the sign blazoned across the door, which said: "Abandon Hope, All Ye Who Enter Here!"

Inside was what it was like for all non-union employees. It was the same for us in there: hopeless. No matter how good our arguments, no matter how keen and concise our points, no matter what. In fact, I often felt it didn't matter at all what we said inside.

Management was like Fox News without the excitement. Rush Limbaugh in monotone. O'Reilly without O'Reilly. What was maintained was the consummate ability to disregard real life and conjure up facts from some alternate reality. No matter what we said or asked for, the answer was, "No". For instance, at times, there might be one guard to cover up to twenty (yes twenty!) galleries. But any request to even look into this problem was immediately squelched. Despite the near impossibility of preventing any of the numerous problems we were paid to prevent, and in spite of the wear and tear on a guard, the answer was always, "We appreciate your concern—NO." If they even bothered to think up reasons why not (and often they didn't), those reasons, ever and always, had nothing to do with the reality and dangers that guards daily encountered.

It went on for days and weeks and months. Really, on our side, there was only one true strategy in there: Keep it going. We waited for the outside magic. Real magic. Our magic. There were real people out there—and we had real issues to tell them.

The problem for management was that they had to "bargain in good faith," or at least, *appear* to bargain in good faith. Otherwise the union could accuse them of bargaining in bad faith.

They had to actually respond to our proposals in a way that appeared to actually be responding. When we made our proposals, they had to move their positions in what seemed to be a reasonable manner. Because if we could prove they were bargaining in BAD FAITH, that would go BAD for them. Even the neutered National Labor Relations Board would be forced to call them to task.

We would ask for all kinds of information. And they had to supply it to us. But that was all a game. Dull, but a game. On their side the goal was to give us as little as absolutely possible but to make it seem reasonable.[6] We were generally just stalling for time. We weren't going to score many points inside, if any. But we could give ourselves more time to make it hot for management outside with our leafleting and media campaigns and demonstrations, etc., and the public reaction from them.[7]

Actually, you could kind of tell how well we were doing outside by the increased movement on their part or lack of it. Or by their anxiety to end it. On the other hand, sometimes, when things were going bad for them, it would be their turn to stall, hoping our people would tire out. That was when McCarthy would say to me, "Ramp it up!"

If management could have kept the whole process in that dismal room, safe from leafleting, demonstrations and the media, and if they hadn't had to worry about that good faith thing, well, then, we would have seen how these corporate giants can run a business, er, Museum. On the other hand, we got a chance to show them how a good union runs a campaign.

26

Power goes to two poles—to those who've got the money And those who've got the people.

--Saul Alinsky

NEGOTIATIONS II: INSIDE THE CAUCUS ROOM

There is another aspect of negotiations that takes place neither in the dismal room nor outside in demonstrations. This is in the side rooms where the team would gather during negotiations to discuss management proposals, counter proposals, or lack of proposals, or where we might adjourn when things got knotty or bogged down.

Union members Russell Gilfoy, Mary Berry and Marilyn Leung at a caucus.

By and large, our negotiating teams were great groups, men and women, gay and straight, Asian, African American, Latino and many other ethnic backgrounds. Each one deserves a medal for spending long hours listening to the B.S. that management offers up, much of it either insulting or boring. But we needed to get out of the bargaining room and just talk to each other and get away from that stifling atmosphere.

When we were in the caucus room, waiting for them to respond to our latest proposal, it would usually take them hours to come up with some piddling sum or some insulting and demeaning answer to some request we had made. Or on the other hand, we might be there having to respond to their latest proposal or request. But in that setting, we got to know each other a little better or maybe we were able to let off some steam or just be bored for a while.

This is when the team would have discussions of all kinds, not always to do with negotiations. This is where we had our major back and forth with McCarthy and with each other. Sometimes, there were huge disagreements, sometimes lighthearted joking. Here we would temper our positions or perhaps expand them, ponder over management, express anger, frustration or puzzlement.

People like Gary Lombard or myself would usually take the extreme position. Members like Russel Gilfoy or Don Cusack would most often stand up for a more measured approach. This was also where McCarthy would regale us with his war stories, such as tales about attorneys, like a certain Jim Lovejoy, who he had often crossed swords with and who were, according to him, much worse even than Scott Faust, the lawyer for the Museum.

Russel Gilfoy might tell us a story from his days as an art and drama teacher at Millis High School, maybe even about starting the first teachers' union. Katie O'Brien was apt to make some wry comment on a subject dear to her heart, more often than not on the foibles of masculinity. Marilyn Leung would often tell us of her latest acting gig. The last and biggest was a part in a Matt Damon movie. Lisa would do a little trash talking about one thing or another. Or she might discuss one of Boston's sports teams with Paul McCarthy.

McCarthy listening to some feedback at a caucus. (You can see some members reflected in the mirror behind him.)

John Storrow was usually laid back, but now and again he would surprise us with strongly held opinions, exclaiming "You can say that again!" Gary Lombard might express his ideas for some extreme action—which was squelched by everyone else. But he might do it by himself anyway. Mary Berry was new and shy but she would often ask interesting questions about what was going on or why management was doing this or that. But I think it was there that I first learned about her little cosmetics business. Jim Kowalski was at once the gentlest one there but also, I felt, he had the deepest emotional reactions. "How could they do that!"

Russell Gilfoy and Mary Berry, during a caucus.

Jerome Ware might interject when things got a little out of hand: "Calm down, everyone. This is business." Don Cusack was often quiet. But he was only waiting for just the right moment to express an important observation. John Moore was mild mannered and somewhat quirky then. He might tell us about his experience at Dance Camp. Later, he became a dedicated and very intense Socialist.

Edwin Jimenez was the shocker. He often acted strange and suspicious. We didn't trust him—with good reason. Two thirds of the way he turned coat and took a supervisor's job from management. Who knows what he had told them?

McCarthy, to his credit, was good at getting the tenor of where the team was at and taking in feedback on how to express this to management. He would make sure he got input from all of us if possible. Then back to the dismal room.

We've got a little message that will shake your corporate suites
You may own the company, but it's we who own the streets.

--from *Union Warriors* by Steve Suffett

NEGOTIATIONS III: IN THE WORKPLACE AND THE STREETS

It was always necessary to keep the troops fired up. As I have said, it was absolutely essential for them to feel an important part of the process (and keep that up for the whole campaign) and to inspire them to participate in the demonstrations in order to convince management to come to terms. It was vital to express things in a way that the members understood just how important it was for them to come out and leaflet, picket and demonstrate. I cannot overstate how sensitive and subtle, and how delicate it was, this process of keeping the members informed. It was, perhaps, the most significant part of McCarthy's dictum to do the real talking outside of the bargaining room.

It was here that the members were kept in the loop, actively drawn in and inspired (so we hoped). The alternative could be disastrous should the members feel they were being passed by and ignored, creating huge divisions. If successful, unlooked for help would come from unexpected people. And it was here that the tide was often turned.

Below are a few examples taken from our security guard newsletter, The Security Blanket, printed before, during and after our contract campaigns. The object, as stated above, is to find out what our members want us to negotiate for in the contract,[1] then to let them know what is going on, to keep morale up during the long campaign and, finally, to let everyone know that it was worth all the struggle, by congratulating ourselves for getting a really good contract:

Preparing for our second contract as an independent union.

Our Issues

We care about our jobs and we care about the Museum:

Management has taken away many of our jobs. We will not sit silently and let them do this. We will speak out.

Management is going to spend hundreds of millions on buildings and nothing on us. We will not let them do this quietly. We will speak out.

Management wants to take away many of our benefits including overtime. We will not just let them do this. We will speak out.

Management has cut coverage to dangerous levels. We won't let them do this without speaking out.

Management has taken away all pay raises from their other workers. We will not let them do that to us.

These are issues which we deeply care about. This is why we are leafleting on the streets and letting management know we are strong and organized.

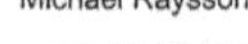
Michael Raysson

The contract campaign has started,
but we want to be sure that all our members understand
what are the issues for which we're fighting.

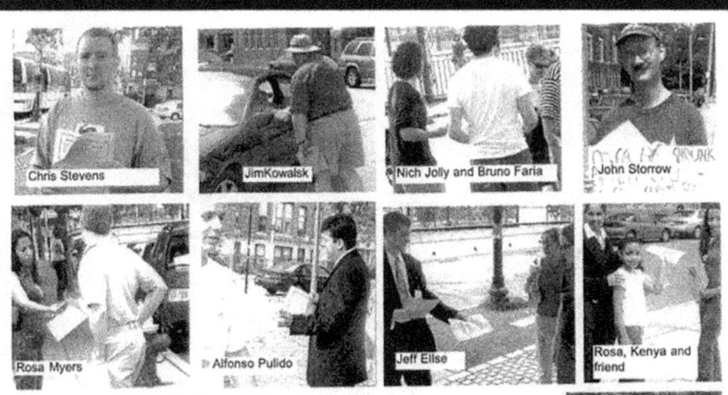

Why We Leaflet

Leafleting is one of the best ways for a Union to communicate with the public. It is a tradition which goes back to the leaders of the American Revolution, who communicated their message in the very same way. We are personally out there on the street sharing our issues, problems and hardships with our employer's customers and patrons. Many of these people are members and they seriously care about how the museum is run. They can and will bring pressure on management to listen to our position.

MFA management does not live in a vacuum. This pressure and adverse publicity makes it much more difficult for them to continue such policies. The more united we are and the more effective the leafleting campaign, the more power we have to bargain with management to get better wages and working conditions.

Union workers are protected in leafleting. An individual worker does not have this protection. They can be fired or otherwise disciplined. Only by working together in a Union can we speak up without fear or intimidation.

Michael Raysson

Further, we want them to understand the importance of leafleting in order to win those issues.

Support for our cause from the community

MFA Director...
MALCOLM ROGERS
MAKES
$500,000 A YEAR
SO WHY CAN'T HE
GIVE HIS WORKERS A
LIVING WAGE

Mr. Rogers,

My wife and I recently visited the MFA and while waiting in line to enter, we had a conversation with some of your employees.These people really and truly love their MFA security jobs and have a great interest in what they do. I'm sure their wages are a drop in a bucket compared to your half million dollar salary, but they depend on their check just as much, if not more than you. While you could (and really probably should) stand to take a pay cut, these people are surviving week to week, like most working class families these days, and the impact of a pay cut on their lives is devastating.

If the plan is to screw these people over and eventually replace them, then you should be ashamed of yourself.The elimination of decent full time jobs with healthcare is one of the greatest cancers in our country right now.Think about what your life would be like if you were in their position today. You are fortunate enough to be in a postion of being able to make decisions that have a huge impact on these peoples' lives and livelihoods by doing the right thing.

Let these people do the job they love in the place they love and make a real difference where it really matters....

DO THE RIGHT THING.
Thank you.

Sincerely,
Stephen Cooke

Union Donated

The members need to see that the public is actually responding to our outside efforts by writing and emailing their support.

Dear Mr. Rogers,

As an employment attorney who represents employees and as a long time MFA member, I was most disturbed to read that the MFA is paying its employees. Wal-Mart wages, cutting benefits, and attempting to convert its full time security work force into part time, low wage positions. Paying the Museum staff living wages and providing benefits should be a priority over new buildings and raises for highly paid administrators.

I regularly receive appeals for money from the MFA, often asking me for hundreds of dollars. I am most disturbed to learn that, while I am asked for such large donations, the security guards are barely making it from week to week and that the MFA is attempting to cut their wages and benefits even further. As I'm sure you are aware, Boston is one of America's most expensive cities in which to live. People who make six figure incomes can barely afford to buy a two bedroom condominium in the Boston metro area. Your employees are not disposable widgets. They provide a valuable service. They keep the Museum running and secure. They are more important than paying hundreds of millions for new structures or increasing the salaries of a few to stratospheric levels. Most of all, they are your fellow human beings.They should be paid living wages.

I certainly hope that the MFA, which provides such a valuable experience for the people of Boston, will pay its workers a living wage. I will have extreme difficulty continuing to support the MFA with my membership and contributions (which stretch my budget) if I learn that Museum employees are being paid wages upon which you would not want anyone in your family to live on.

Sincerely,

Rebecca G. Pontikes

Dear friends:

I sent this e-mail to Mr. Rogers today. Good luck in your struggle!

Dear Mr. Rogers:

I was aghast and appalled to learn about your inhumane treatment of the security guard staff. They need a living wage and FULL benefits, not cuts in wages and benefits.

The greatest art in this life is the fair, equitable and just treatment of our fellow human beings. All of the art in the MFA is not worth a fraction of a human being, the ultimate artwork of our Creator. Remember that and let that guide you in your negotiations with labor at all times.

As a member and devotee of the MFA, I am holding you accountable to do the right thing.

Sincerely yours,
George Milowe, M.D.

Below is a copy of the letter I sent by e-mail to Malcolm Rogers. Best wishes to all the guards involved in this effort.

Dear Mr. Rogers,
On a recent visit to the museum, I was surprised to observe a number of security guards distributing fliers on the sidewalk leading to the West Wing entrance. When I approached and asked their purpose, I was dismayed to find they had to resort to petitioning support for their efforts to obtain reasonable job security, wages and benefits from this great institution, with its plans underway for huge expansion.
I have been going to the Museum of Fine Arts for more than six decades and have always found the guards courteous and helpful. Some of them I've come to know by sight, since they have served there for so many years. The cut-back of full-time gallery posts and the uncertainty of the guards who are still employed is appalling. The escalation of admission and membership costs makes a visit to MFA far less accessible than it was, even taking inflation into account. The museum's treatment of these valuable employees makes it far less pleasant, as well. I hope these concerns will be addressed and a more just and fair resolution will result.
Sincerely,

(Ms.) Cal Kolbe

Even more instances of public for our members to see.

Finally, after all the work, and against huge odds, we have gotten a great contract. Notice that even other larger unions are amazed

We were able to do so well. The second article relates to the work still ahead of us to get a full union shop. (We did.)

SECURITY BLANKET

Vol. 2 No. 2 THE VOICE OF THE MFA INDEPENDENT SECURITY UNION March 27, 1996

HOW SWEET IT IS!
CONGRATULATIONS TO US!
JOB WELL DONE!

One day after we ratified our contract, I went to a labor meeting. Present were Union officers and members of the Teamsters, the Service Employees Union, the Auto Workers, the Electrical Workers and many more. They asked me how our contract came out. When I told them what we got, there was a roar of applause like nothing else at that meeting and everyone congratulated me on getting an exceptionally great contract.

The same enthusiastic appreciation came to our consultant, Paul McCarthy from Union leaders at a Labor Guild dinner. A head of one of the major unions said, "I wish I could bring a contract like that to my people". Many other comments were equally enthusiastic.

All in all, knowledgeable people in labor were amazed that a small independent union won such an excellent contract from the powerful MFA.

Understand that downsizing and take-aways are the rule for workers today. And understand that the Museum itself was intent to deal with us in a like manner. This was a victory of activism, persistance and hard work that bucked the trend. (The New York Times had a seven part article on corporations whose workers had fallen the other way.)

So this is a time for celebration - and the realization that if we all work together 100% we can do twice as good next time.

Michael Raysson

Yes Yes Yes Yes Yes Yes Yes

Closing the Gap

ALL NEWLY HIRED GUARDS

We are still able to have a UNION SHOP.
Each member who opts for the union brings us closer.
All new employees must become members.

EACH YES CLOSES THE GAP.

WHY A UNION SHOP?

People, mainly management, who want to break the power of unions like to tell us that only in an open shop where workers have a right to choose to pay dues and belong to a union do we have true freedom. It sounds good but the argument is a total deception. It is the same as arguing that we should have the voluntary option to pay taxes or not. Not even the most libertarian of politicians would suggest such a thing. Obviously all the deadbeats would immediately cease paying. They would get the same benefits as the "fools" who continued to pay. Most everyone likes a free ride. In the mean time the government would soon run down and cease to exist and all protection and benefits for the common man and woman would be lost. We would be at the mercy of the rich and powerful and also the unlawful.

The exact same is true of a open shop. What they don't tell you is that everyone gets the same benefits whether they pay or not. (It's surprising how quickly those

28

You will never forget the empathy and the good fights.
--from *Retirement of a Unionist*
by David G. Hurlburt

IN RETROSPECT

In retrospect, the actions of the United Plant Guard Workers leadership (or lack of it) were the best thing that could have happened to us. Had we continued under them, even in a best-case scenario, we would not have felt the empowerment which working in a true union environment brings. Basically, we did it by ourselves. In "by ourselves," I include our consultant and mentor, Paul McCarthy and our lawyer, Bob Schwartz. I believe little is possible without a real mentor, and a good lawyer makes the playing field just a little more level.

A small union working against one of the most powerful institutions in Boston was able to mount successful campaign after successful campaign. We did this without being overseen by any powerful national or international union. In fact, all of our members and officers were under the employ of the Boston Museum of Fine Arts and subject to their intervention and threat in all phases of our working life. Generally, we had no paid union officers. We were dependent upon the Museum and whatever other side job (or jobs) we might find for our sustenance. Thus the degree of difficulty was extreme.

There were a few times when I discussed with Paul McCarthy the possibility of connecting up with or working in a larger union. "You wouldn't like it", he said. "All the autonomy and freedom you have here would disappear."

I must add that all the indications were that the corporate overseers of the Museum seriously wanted to rid themselves of our union. Apparently, one of the jobs expected of a Director of Security was to help diminish the power of the Union or get rid of it altogether. I have mentioned that every time we succeeded in our campaigns (with one exception), the director of security was fired soon after. That one exception was around the time that the corporate powers of the Museum were putting together the blueprint for a high-powered building campaign, so perhaps the pain in the neck guards faded into the background for a while.

The lessons we learned were lessons learned under fire and on the front lines, against a powerful and determined enemy.

29

You go to the boss and the boss would yell,
"Before I raise your pay, I'd see you all in hell"
Well, he's puffing a big seegar, feeling mighty slick
'Cause he thinks he's got your union licked
Well, he looks out the window and what does he see
But a thousand pickets and they all agree
He's a bastard, unfair, slave driver,
Bet he beats his wife!

--from *Talking Union*
by Lee Hays, Millard Lampell and Pete Seeger

THE UNION IS THE CONSCIENCE OF THE MUSEUM

My observation of the Museum after the corporate takeover was that for all intents and purposes, it was run like a small dictatorship or a monarchy. If you went along with the program, I suppose it was a "nice" dictatorship. If you didn't, like Jonathan Fairbanks (See the chapter, *The Boston Massacre)*, you were out of there on the seat of your pants. And just forget freedom of speech. Anyway, that's how I looked at it.

From my angle of vision the chronology of the corporate takeover at the Boston Museum of Fine Arts went like this: Part one was the gradual takeover of the Board of Trustees by corporate CEOs in the high-end money investment field in the 1980s and 90s. Part two was the "retirement" of Tom Manning as director of security in 1989 and his job being taken by State Police sergeant William P. McAuliffe. Part three was the "resignation" of Alan Shestack in 1994 and his place being taken by Malcolm A. Rogers, formerly the deputy director of the

London Portrait Gallery. With these changes, the foundation blocks were in place for the corporate blueprint to go into action.

While Malcolm Rogers was not the originator of that plan, he was the man who carried it out. As such, he became the face of the Museum for the next twenty years. In this way my relationship with Malcolm and the relationship of the Union at large was established.

As far as minority presence, certainly for African Americans, in the upper echelons of the Corporate Museum there were none. Malcolm had made a pretense of reopening the Huntington Avenue door, which pointed in the direction of the minority neighborhood of Roxbury. In point of fact, it would seem to have merely been a pretext to get more minority customers past the turnstiles. Because, except for a few Asian American curators in the Asian Art Department, the Museum remained absolutely lily white in all but the Cleaning, Utilities and Security Departments, as long as I was there.

There was one black consultant, Barry Gaithers, who was the director over at the African American Museum. Barry was said to also be a curator at the Museum, but I saw him there only once or twice a year. As far as I know, he had nothing to do with the departments at the main place.

Mostly Malcolm's British charm brought him adulation from donors, from the media and from his superiors on the Board. We were the only ones in the Museum who did not go along with the program, so you can imagine how he felt toward us. Why, we even had our own Newsletter, *The Security Blanket,* where we regularly expressed our uncensored opinions, and included in it piercing criticisms of Malcolm and the Museum (along with cultural articles, member's artwork, writings and poetry, and news of all sorts related to our union.). The union brought a different face of Malcolm Rogers to the light of day, to the public at large, to the patrons of the Museum and even, at times, to the same adoring media. Malcolm, thin-skinned as he was, hated this. He hated the Union and he hated me. All his years he attempted to rid the Museum of us and me.

Malcolm only made one direct communication to us during negotiations, and that was in 1995, when he started out offering us a five-cent raise. Then the Museum lawyer, Scott Faust, stepped up at the beginning of the second bargaining session, saying, "*Malcolm Rogers wants you to know that you should not expect anything. Only people who make money for the Museum should expect raises.*" I was shocked and everyone on our bargaining team was shocked. Of course, we knew they felt that way, but to come out and bald-facedly proclaim it was amazing. It was a statement of what the Boston Museum Of Fine Arts, supposedly one of the world's great cultural institutions, stood for in the new corporate playing field and their disdain for us and all the others who did not bring them money.

In the 2005-2006 contract campaign, Malcolm aimed to take our benefits away from us, just like he had done to all his non-union employees. He publicly stated that he would "never give in to this union." The campaign went on for a year and half. One time in that campaign I was outside leafleting with a bunch of other guards. Malcolm was making a special appearance inside, talking to the patrons. I handed out leaflets to a couple of women and talked to them a while, telling them how Malcolm wanted to take away our benefits and how he otherwise made things greatly uncomfortable for us. The women were concerned and said they would go inside and express their displeasure to Malcolm. They did so and came back. "Well, what did he reply?" I asked them. "He said that as long as you and these other people are part of the union, he will never, ever give you anything." While he was determined not to give in, we were more determined. In both cases I have mentioned above, from the campaigns of 1995 and 2005-6, we got good contracts anyway.

I don't think Malcolm ever considered how his policies affected the workers of the Museum, especially those low wage earners who just got by from week to week. There was only one time that I can remember in which he expressed contrition for what he did, and that is when he laid off twenty-one employees in 1995. However, he blamed it on an economic downturn. But those were false tears or mock tears or lying tears, because, in reality, the Museum had had one of its best economic years ever. (See Chapter 33 on "Media, last paragraph), in which the full story is told of how we discovered and exposed MFA management in this Machiavellian episode.)

From our side, any strategy based on gaining Malcolm's sympathy or appealing to his better side was a waste of energy and time. Nonetheless, we treated him (and the Museum) with nuance. When our demonstrations, leaflets, petitions, etc. resulted in their changing their behavior or policies for the better, we reacted with varying degrees of appreciation. When they insisted on continuing their repressive ways, we continued (and ramped up, if possible) our resistance. But Malcolm Rogers was ever and always the one we held accountable.

It helped that he was extremely thin skinned. Once in a leafleting campaign we handed out little stickers the size of a postage stamp for the patrons to stick or pin on their clothing. That little sticker told how much Malcolm made (a lot!) and how little we low wage earners were given (darn little!). Malcolm was in Japan, but he heard about it and apparently went ballistic. Well, somehow that got back to me. So instead of a tiny sticker, I had a twenty-foot sign made with the same information. Roy Williams, the guard in the coatroom by one of the doors, saw Malcolm start to leave and then look out and notice the huge banner. "That man turned right around as fast as he could and headed for the other door!" said Roy, with a huge smile.

When I heard that, I had another banner like that one made (with the help of the Carpenters' Union), except this time it was thirty feet long. And I had it positioned at the other door.

Many of the guards entered the Museum believing in beauty and artistic creativity, having labored as an artist or studied art history. For us, at least at the beginning, the Museum was the Temple of Beauty. Art was a noble profession, and we shared our worship with the patrons who came through the door.

In a sense, Malcolm was a glorified pitchman hired by the Board of Trustees to sell their product and get rid of those who stood in their way. He kicked my favorite curator (and the favorite of many others also) Cornelius Vermeule out the back door of the Museum after almost fifty years of service. The prevailing view of most of the staff was, Vermeule was fired for being openly friendly with many guards and writing regularly in our newsletter.

Here, an article by Constance Gorfinkel, which appeared in the March 4, 1995 Quincy *Patriot-Ledger* newspaper and was reprinted in part in our newsletter, under the Headline, *Malcolm Bristled, (forgive the typos)*:

> Sitting in shirtsleeves in his airy office at the MFA, Rogers appeared somewhat more tense last week than he was during an interview last summer, but he appeared supremely confident in his changes. that attitude is quite different than the gallows humor expressed by staff members who pass one another in the waiting area outside his office."I'm not supposed to talk about it," said one woman when asked to describe her feelings about the staff cuts Rogers announced two weeks ago. "It's too bad you can't read minds," she added.
>
> Rodgers is philosophical about what he believes is the temporary gloom caused by those cuts--83 out of 480 staff positions, in an effort to save $3.4 million in the next fiscal year's operating budget of $23.5 milion.
>
> "There's bound to be a period of mouning," he said "But I'm not going to allow an atmosphere of gloom to set in. People have made their sacrificed so that we can move ahead positively. That's the vital thing."
>
> Rogers bristled, though, when asked to react to aletter sent by the museum guards' union, which has filed a complaint with the National Labor Relations Board over 10 guard positions cut in the new restructuring.
>
> In the letter, sent to union members, union president Michael Raysson accused Rogers of being hired by the museum to be a hatchet man.
>
> To say that statement "is unfair is a mild way of putting it. It is untrue, completelely untrue. I was brought in to be director here, to manage the institution. I was not given an agenda by anybody. I've been left to my own devices and I've worked here with senior staff to bring about a practical solution to our problems, which I presented (for the first time) to the trustees yesterday.
>
> "All the time, what I've been doing I've been discussing with the chairman and the president of the board of trustees. But I've been left with complete autonomy."
>
> Rogers said museum security would not be compromised by the guard cuts, because part-time guards will be hired to replace the full-timers.

The union stood in the way of the corporate string pullers. Unlike the individual staff members he so easily removed, the union had certain rights under the law. But most important, we had the right to bring Malcolm's unscrupulous ways of doing business to the eyes of the public. We could embarrass him, which embarrassed the Museum.

Much of the rest of the staff, especially the curatorial staff, felt much the same way about Malcolm as we did. After all, curators in the corporate mold were just "replaceable cogs in a wheel," to quote Malcolm. But what could they do? They were afraid to even make a peep. The one exception was Ted Stebbins, the former curator of American Art at the MFA. But he had to quit to speak his piece after the Boston Massacre. Quoting from Patti Hartigan's article (see above): "[Stebbins] was irate that his colleagues were treated like 'criminals'. "It was really an outrageous thing to do," ... "It was more than a shot across the bow. It was a real wounding of the curatorial staff."

But we could roar, not only as the union, but also the public whom we encouraged to call, write, email and, ultimately petition, Malcolm and the Museum.

The union was the conscience of the Museum and of Malcolm. A conscience doesn't work by being nice. With corporate CEO's and the like, it can almost never work that way. I tried being nice to them once. They seemed to like that less than when I was out and out fighting against the Museum. Perhaps they just preferred that Malcolm take the heat and that they remain invisible.

At a meeting of the Museum Board of Trustees I handed out a letter to each of them, stating very nicely and politely how we could mutually work out our problems. Board membe Peter Lynch, the famous investment advisor and author, apparently was so incensed by my polite little letter that he tried to get me fired (according to what one supervisor reported back to me). In the battle with corporate leaders, you are dealing with guys who didn't get there by being nice.

Those of us who worked for the union at the Museum walked a tightrope. Unlike many unions that have professional officers from the outside, we were all on the inside, employed by the employer whom we often fought against. In that way, Malcolm and the Museum had a power over us only nullified by our power with the public and the everyday power that a union still affords, especially to officers. We made sure that Malcolm felt the pressure from our side.

In my last campaign at the Museum, Malcolm said he would never give in to this union. Miraculously, the union made him "eat those words." But it was not by being nice and it took a year and a half. It was achieved only by constantly increasing that pressure on the Museum. That was a huge victory for us and a huge defeat for the bosses.

A friend will tell you what you want to hear. A mentor will tell you what you need to hear.

--John DiLemme

WORKING WITH A MENTOR

When Paul McCarthy met us at the little middle eastern restaurant down the street from the Boston Museum of Fine Arts, it seems to me that he saw hooking up with the security guards at the Museum as a great chance, one on which he was willing to make a huge gamble. The hook, and an enticing one for Paul, was the possibility of engaging in battle with a celebrated world class cultural institution. It was a place that he and his wife Susan had long enjoyed as patrons. For this opportunity he was willing to put in with an inexperienced hardscrabble group of widely diverse security guards who seemingly had little chance of winning the battle ahead of them. So tempting was this hook of a chance to help that he even entered into a contract with them knowing that there wasn't enough money to pay him for the first year.

On that foundation, McCarthy became our consultant and mentor, and a fruitful relationship it was. Certainly, we would not have won without him, in this the first of many successful battles with the Museum. Ultimately, he got paid and rewarded many times over, while we learned the ins and outs of one of the great professions, union organizing (although mostly we did it for free).

Few things are more enjoyable than strategizing with a knowledgeable mentor. Few things are more necessary for a beginning union. Entering at the grassroots level, as we did, generally means that you are sitting ducks for a corporate management which is altogether ready with both tricks and power to take full advantage of the innocent and guileless. So, it was our good fortune to get a great mentor.

That's McCarthy (far right), me (in the middle) and the president of the Engineers' Local (on the left). It was rare for McCarthy to go out on forays with us (he wanted us to learn on our own), such as this one reaching out to another union.

Because I was mentored by Paul, I learned to be pragmatic rather than dogmatic or ideological. Once, I was on a panel with Peter Schumann, founder of Bread and Puppet Theater at the local Cambridge YMCA. Bread and Puppet Theater is a socially active group based in Vermont. At every performance, homemade bread and dip are handed out free, and "cheap art" goes up for sale. When I went to see them up in Vermont, I expected a funky hippy-type performance. But while Hippy-ness might have been there, it was beautiful, masterful art of the highest order. Their subject matter embraces important social causes of the day and they tour extensively.

Listening to my experiences, Peter said, approvingly (in his German accent), "I like hunion organicers who vin." At least partly, that quality came from McCarthy's tutelage. Paul was not after "feel good" victories that actually got you nothing, and which often lost you something.

Saul Alinsky

He had studied under Saul Alinsky, the famous organizer from Chicago. My neighbor, who went to the University of Chicago, tells this story: Alinsky came there for a talk. My neighbor went. A few days before, the University of Chicago football team had lost a football game, 72-0. But the school paper came out and called it a moral victory. Alinsky saw the paper, and in his talk, he said, "I am not a believer in moral victories for organizers!"

I have said that McCarthy was big on Sun Tzu. Therefore, his advice was often to hold back on the attack. "Let them think you are going to do it, and fear what you *might do,"* he would say, "Once you have done it, then they know, *'Oh, that wasn't so bad.'*" He would inevitably finish with, "It's not what you have that matters, but what they think you have."

Generally, it was not a problem to get the guards to hold back on the attack as people who come to work in a place like the Boston Museum of Fine Arts are not apt to be overly aggressive. But then there was Gary Lombard. Gary did not always follow Sun Tzu. And that would get him in trouble with McCarthy (if McCarthy found out). For instance, once Gary discovered where the ex-wife of John Stanley (the Assistant Director of the Museum) lived. They were in a bitter court battle at the time. Gary would go to her house and leave swaths of our leaflets, especially ones that were critical of Stanley, at her doorway. One morning after one of Gary's soirees, Stanley came into our bargaining meeting madder than a hive of threatened hornets. For a while, he was impossible to deal with. Eventually, he got over it.

On the other side of holding back, when we had exerted ourselves to the utmost, he would often exhort us to do more. "Easy for you to say!" I would reply. "Well, what you have done hasn't worked so far. You have to do more. (And better)!"

Looking back, I agree with McCarthy (generally) that it is better to hold back. But I also feel that having management knowing the threat that something like a surprise attack from someone like Gary could happen at any time wasn't a bad thing, either.

McCarthy loved to tell "War Stories." Fortunately, he was a great raconteur. He would often regale us with a few of his tales when we adjourned to the caucus room in negotiations and at once break up the depressive and melancholic atmosphere coming from management's proposals and counter proposals.

For instance, if we were going into a contract ratification meeting with a good contract, he would always tell the story of a teachers' union he had worked for. They had had a tremendously difficult fight with their management. But in the end, they had won everything they had wanted except for one thing. So the president of the union starts the meeting with, "We didn't get such and such, but..." Before the president can say anything else, the meeting erupted. Chairs were flying. There were fist fights. To this day, that union is irrevocably split over that one little issue.

McCarthy always warned me not to do the same. "Tell them all the positive things you got in the contract." Every contract, he told the same story.

McCarthy, teaching at the Boston Labor Guild. In this case, two of his students, Rodney Hewes (second from the left) and Russell Gilfoy (fourth from the left), are from our union.

On the whole, talking strategy with McCarthy was one of the great delights of union building. The more difficult, the better. In the beginning we sometimes did have our knock-down, drag out battles. But we gradually learned how to deal and communicate with each other with joy and respect, as described above.

McCarthy taught us how to rally the troops when they had temporarily lost their spirit. How to deal with management when they refused to recognize our union rights. When to go out on small sorties of one or two or three people to leaflet a corporate sponsor of the Museum. Or when to do nothing. What would be our message for the contract campaign at hand?

On the latter, McCarthy was adamant about staying on message. I remember how upset he would get if we lost our focus. "Stick to your message. Stick to your message." Especially when talking to the media, "Stick to your message. Don't go off on personal tangents." Everything we did had to center on "our issues." And he would add, "Don't get involved in other people's battles.

At first, McCarthy was the voice of experience and I was the neophyte. Gradually, it became a conversation of equals, to a point. The student always needs to have a special place of respect for their mentor from beginning to end. That's the way it works.

My relationship with McCarthy lasted fourteen years. We still see and talk with each other about present politics and the old days at the Museum. But now I can add war stories of my own.

31

He will win who knows when to fight and when not to fight.

--Sun Tzu

SMART AND DUMB IDEAS

Sometimes, I would come up with what seemed to me a great idea and I would relate it to McCarthy. "Well, that's great," he would say, "but are the troops with you on this?" If I answered in the negative, he would then say something like, "Well, it's going to be awful lonely on the battlefield against management all by yourself." Further, he would question me whether that was something that the other guards even wanted. Did I even know what they wanted? Had I even bothered to ask?

At other times, I came up with ideas that would humiliate or embarrass the Museum—or Malcolm Rogers, himself. "Yes," McCarthy would say, "that will make them look bad. But what will you get out of it for your people? Is it just going to make you feel good (while getting management good and mad and just waiting to get even with you)?" Fortunately, in these cases, I usually listened to McCarthy.

I often used to look at the union work as something like walking on the tightrope backwards while juggling, without a net. It is a metaphor, of course. The metaphor deepens when we consider the composition of that high wire. The wire must be made of grassroots. The moment the union high wire artist feels those grassroots under foot, he or she knows they are safe. No matter how high it might seem that they are, in reality, their feet are on the ground. Conversely, if the wire is otherwise and the union artist fails to feel those good old grassroots under foot, they know (or should know) they are ready for a fall, and a mighty big one.

Now, if it wasn't immediately obvious, one way or the other, about those great ideas I had, I learned another thing from McCarthy: Bring it up to the union executive board. Let them decide. Let them take responsibility. Let them contribute. There our *"eminence grise" Don Cusack* could give his wise counsel, expressing caution or agreement as the case might be. Or our young genius, Josh Lyons, might come up with some angle everyone else had missed. Or Marilyn Leung might step forward with a few of her creative thoughts on the subject. And so on...*That* really *was* a safety net. And it was the *union way: the people all working together* or *The People United Can Never Be Defeated.* It saved many a potentially fatal fall.

Having said all that stuff above, things still were not always cut and dried. For instance, in a small independent union with limited resources and where many of its members lived week to week, it was a dumb idea to go on strike. However, it was not a dumb idea to let management *think* you would go on strike. Here, McCarthy, in his SunTzu incarnation would give out, "What matters is not what you are, but what the enemy *thinks* you are."

The *secret* here is the ability to appear *as if* you are going to do something or that you *can do* something that, in reality, you have no intention or, possibly, ability, to do. Smoke and mirrors.

At times, we gave the appearance that we might strike, or that we might have Occupy Boston waiting to occupy the Museum, or that we might do crazy things at the blockbuster Winslow Homer show. We were dumbfounded when the Museum lawyer came before our bargaining team one time, asking us if we were really

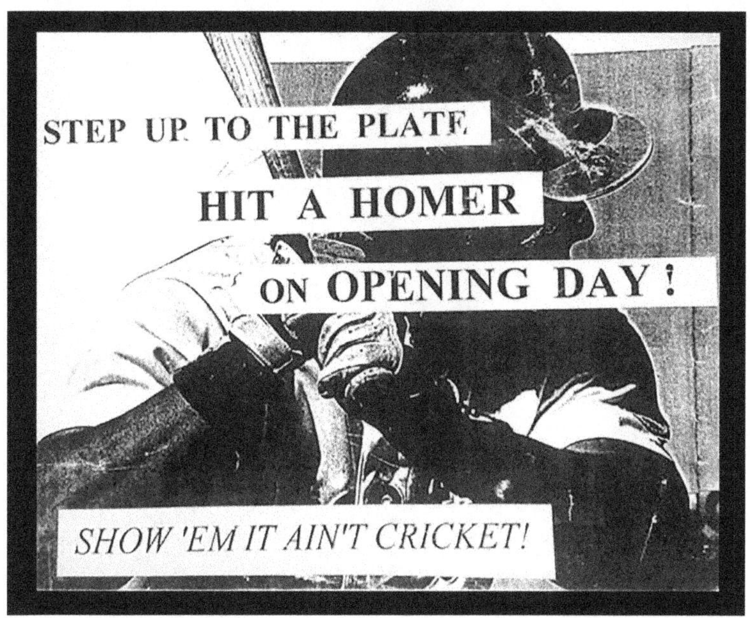
STEP UP TO THE PLATE
HIT A HOMER
ON OPENING DAY !
SHOW 'EM IT AIN'T CRICKET!

This is the leaflet created by Robert Nason when the Museum was having an exhibition of paintings by Winslow Homer, a famous nineteenth century American artist. The Museum thought we meant it literally. We didn't, but we let that sit with them for a while

going to hit Homer's paintings. If one or two of our people leaflet in front of the building where a Museum corporate sponsor was located, the corporate people there will get just as pissed off as if 25 or 30 people were leafleting. And they will call the Museum and tell them so. It is easy to believe that we would do the same thing in front of the trustees' homes, or Malcolm's (and, once or twice, in fact, we did).

If Gary Lombard has done crazy things in the past, it is not difficult to believe we might do even crazier things in the future. The secret is that it is not necessary to actually do it. Or, that it is not necessary to do it on a large scale. Small is beautiful. *Nothing at all* can be even more beautiful.

32

Unions shouldn't run from the media, but reach out to explain their case clearly and forcefully, treating media as they would unfriendly employers whose at least grudging cooperation they win through skillful negotiations or, as a last resort, through public protests, demonstrations and picketing.

--from Labor and the Media by Dick Meister

THE MEDIA

My first experience with a newspaper reporter was an eye opening one. You might say a complete surprise. It was one which in many ways set the tone for all future engagements with the media. We were organizing under UPGWA to bring in the very first labor union in the history of the Boston Museum of Fine Arts. A reporter from the Boston Globe, Patti Hartigan, came to the Museum to cover the story. I was in my gallery, and she came over and introduced herself and began asking questions. It wasn't long before the Museum got wind of this, and along comes the assistant director of security, Jack Burke, who forcibly takes her arm and leads her out of the place.

Later, she made an appointment with me. We met at a restaurant and had a very nice talk. She complained to me, "Not one person from the Museum will talk to me. I can't remember ever having an experience like this!" Meanwhile, we have very pleasant discussion and I tell her all about the guards and our troubles with management. She seemed really interested and took lots of notes. Personally, I was ecstatic. I thought we would get a great story.

A few days later the story came out. It was a large, voluminous "puff piece" for the Museum. I was astounded. I showed it to my wife, who had had plenty of experience with the press as an advocate for immigrants and immigrant rights. "How is this possible?" I cried. "They wouldn't even talk to her! They even kicked her out of the Museum!" "Listen," said my wife, "Who are the people she hobnobs with or would like to hobnob with? Are they security guards or bigwigs at the Museum? Who is going to help her on the ladder to success? And on whose board is the publisher of her paper?"

The publishers of the Boston Globe were perennially trustees of the Museum.

It took a while to learn the ropes of dealing with the media, but as time went on, we did have some success. On one campaign, I remember someone from Jobs with Justice saying that we deserved an award for best media coverage. I always thought we had a compelling story. One trick is getting that story across to the public. Another is getting it across to the media. Besides learning to write a good press release, there is the art of making it seem interesting or enticing enough for the people of the media to make it seem worthwhile to come out and see your demonstration.

Sometimes images have a life of their own. A little sticker the size of a postage stamp ultimately became a thirty foot banner emblazoned with: "Malcolm Rogers makes over $500,000 a year. Why is he taking money away from his low wage workers?" That banner was photographed and the photo was published in the Boston Globe. Just about every article during that campaign also showed a photograph of us demonstrating with that sign.

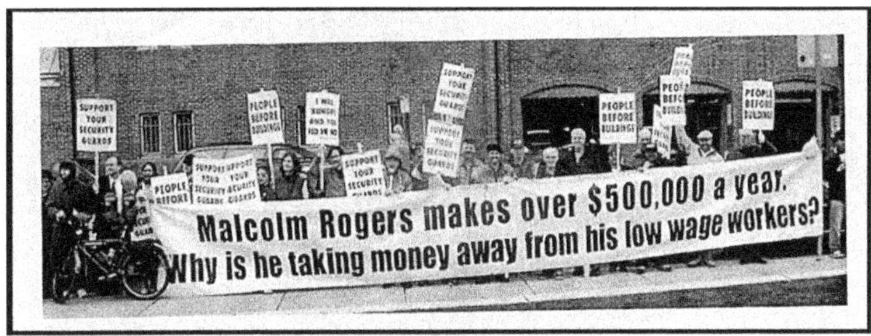

A picture of a group of enthusiastic demonstrators taken with Malcolm's thirty-foot sign mentioned above.

You never know who will or won't be your ally in the media. I was anxious to find one among the liberal columnists in the Boston Globe. I sent a letter to all of them and no one responded. Once again, it was my wife who gave me good advice. "Why not try Steve Bailey? He writes a column on the Financial Page. Just a few weeks ago he wrote a nice story about a labor union."

Steve Bailey, writer of the "Steve Bailey Downtown" column for the Boston Globe, and a legendary newspaperman in Boston.

"Are you kidding? Why would a financial columnist listen to our story?"

Finally, I did write to Steve and he agreed to meet me in front of the Museum. "What's the deal?" he asked. I told him our story, and that was that. He was the best ally in the media I ever had. He regularly put a paragraph or two about us in his column. "Right under the stock prices which the rich board members look at," as my wife described it.

Steve was about objectivity based on fairness and ethics. This immediately put him on our side. He had long since earned his stripes, so he seemed pretty much fearless in his reporting.

The biggest coup, and certainly a huge indication of how devastating a loss of face was for the Museum, came sometime after the Museum had laid off 23 employees, including many guards. Malcolm Rogers cried poor. John Stanley, the assistant director of the Museum, had come before us and told us in his most sincere voice, "How do you think I felt sitting across the table, having to tell someone that they were losing their job?" While this rang entirely untrue to many of us who felt the Museum had other reasons for getting rid of these 23 employees, we had no evidence to back this up.

Well, one night doing my watch guard rounds, I happened to find a memorandum from the Museum's Financial Committee, dated just a few weeks before the lay-offs, lying around. In it, the very same John Stanley told the committee that the Museum had just had one of its best financial years in history, doubling their expected budget. Here, I finally had the smoking gun. I was ecstatic. I went outside and danced in the parking lot. I imagined calling Steve Bailey, as soon as I got home. I did, even though it was late at night. Steve asked, "Do you have an actual copy of that?" "Yes!" "Let me see it." I met him the next day at our usual place in front of the Museum and gave him the copy. He looked it over. "Great!" The following day it was in his column. Two days later, they were putting up new surveillance cameras in the administrative area.

During campaigns, we tried to make our demonstration attractive to the media as well as the public.

Business

THE BOSTON GLOBE FRIDAY, JUNE 17, 2005

STEVE BAILEY

Downtown

Neighborhood news. As the Museum of Fine Arts continues to seek givebacks in a new contract with its security guards, it makes the point to anyone who will listen that these are tough times — even as it is raising hundreds of millions to expand. But what the MFA has been saying in public and private are two different things.

Here is what director Malcolm Rogers said to the staff in June in disclosing 23 layoffs: "These have been tough economic times nationwide. . . . This has required us to examine every expense and to make adjustments appropriate to the long-term interests of the museum."

Here is what deputy director John Stanley told the board in September, according to the board minutes:

"Overall it was an excellent year for the museum, which along with the School of the Museum and the Museum of Fine Arts and Enterprise, ended the year in the black." Stanley reported gains virtually across the board — in assets, investments, giving, and cash. The corporation's "net," as he described it, was $2.4 million — or twice what was budgeted.

A museum spokeswoman says the job cuts were to avoid future deficits, and says $1 million of the surplus went for staff bonuses.

Bailey's column, which exposed the Museum's duplicitous ways for all to see.

This often translated into good photo ops. One time, we dressed up as famous artists, carrying signs appropriate to who they were. Such as: "Leonardo tells the Boston MFA to put things in proper perspective." "Jackson Pollock tells Museum Management, 'Don't Treat Your Workers Like Drips'". This last one was the brainchild of Harry Brill, who taught labor history at Umass at the time. Lately, he has reinvented himself as a labor leader of some importance in Berkeley, California.

The public loved the art work, and the papers got great photographs.

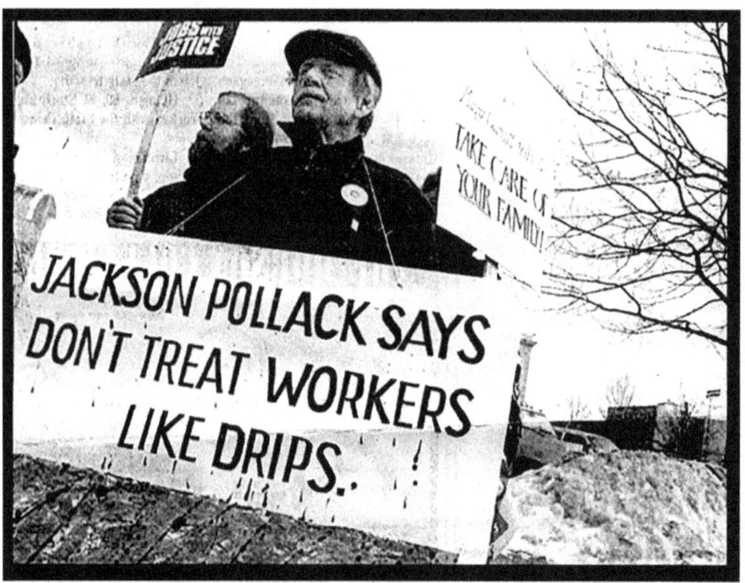

To show the importance that using media at the right place and at the right time can bring, let me just retell this story from the end of my last contract campaign (See Chapter 23). This took place after a year and a half of campaigning without getting management to budge from their pitifully small offers in contract negotiations. Then we had our biggest and most significant demonstration. The very next day, we had an opinion piece of ours, placed front and center in the Boston Globe Op-ed page. In a moment this broke open the stalled negotiations that had seemed to last forever. Two days later, we had an agreement and a successful contract.

In this discussion of media, I cannot forget Patti Hartigan, with whom I began this chapter. Years after I retired, Patti calls me. She is writing an article on Malcolm Rogers, who has recently retired from the Museum. Patti is no longer in the employ of the Boston Globe. She is an established freelance writer and she wants to talk with me. Remembering my first experience, I give her a rather guarded interview. But this time, unfettered by the *Globe*, she wrote an absolutely great piece for the Boston magazine of September 2015. It was titled, *Malcolm Rogers has left the Building*. But it was subtitled, "*Which raises the question: Did he save the MFA? Or ruin it?*" I quote it a number of times in the chapter on "Malcolm, the Union and Me." McCarthy even joked that it was so hard hitting I could have written it.

But most amazing of all, in this article Patti dropped a surprising bombshell: Malcolm Rogers had lost the Museum an astounding $140 million:

"[He] is also leaving behind $140 million in debt, a little-known secret that raises questions about his financial prowess. After more than two decades at the helm of the city's most distinguished museum, he leaves the MFA as one of the most polarizing figures the city's insular art world has ever seen." Patti Hartigan, *Malcolm Rogers has left the Building,* p.92, Boston Magazine, September 2015.

My desire and my anger are contained in this flier.
My voice and my life are contained in this flier.
--from *One Sheet of Flier* by Tetsuro Tanaka

GOOD OLD-FASHIONED LEAFLETS

Leaflets are one of the greatest weapons in the Union arsenal. It's a piece of paper that allows us to meet the public face to face and convey our message to them.

Sometimes, you just hand out the flier to the passing patron. But at other times the patron will question the leafleteer about the message. Then the union member has a chance to express the reason for our demonstrations and their personal feelings about it (how difficult it is to get by, how hard this is for their family, etc.). These interactions can be important conversations and open up a two-way communication between the Union and the Public.

In addition to succinctly expressing our issues, the leaflet often suggests a further way for the patron to express their sympathy and concern to management, by way of phone, email or, even by petition.

Many times, we would personalize our leaflets with pictures of union members, along with a small biography. If relevant, we might even add their family, for many of us were trying to raise a family on our small salary.

Carlos Oviedo discusses our issues with a cyclist who stopped to take a leaflet

Mary Jane McCarty answers the questions of an interested patron

Shirley Monroe talking to a patron

Many patrons would communicate their concern about how we were treated and how important we were to their museum experience.

Imagine the Museum management, which heavily frowned on free unhampered speech inside its precincts, watching an exchange between union members and the public and communicating so many embarrassing facts about them. Thousands of patrons may take the leaflets and carefully read what we have to say. Then, imagine management having to take large amounts of time trying to reply to and explain hundreds of emails and phone calls and shuddering at the comments on the union petition. Add to this the knowledge that director Malcolm Rogers was exceptionally thin skinned.

Here are a couple of samples of responses from patrons, which were communicated to the Museum:

"I am a member of the MFA and I have totally enjoyed my voyages there this past year. Because of a disability, I use a power wheelchair and many of the guards have been both knowledgeable and kind when I was there on my own. These good people are a priceless part of your institution. Shame on you for disregarding them and their livelihoods"

--**Elizabeth Casey** *(from a petition)*

Sir,

I am concerned with the apparent lack of social conscience with the organization of the mfa. I learned that the normal wages, job security and benefits for the lower income employees of the mfa are currently being reconsidered, that a shift is being made to temporary jobs without benefits, as if committed museum personnel are mere waitresses, and all this even though the museum has no solvency issues and there seems to be enough money for a building expansion and for the higher ranking jobs. I would expect that a cultural institution like the mfa would have higher standards than the typical corporate greed that has become more and more prevalent in the US.

I hope you will consider my remarks in your negotiations with the employees of the mfa, and that the museum can not only be proud of its art, but also of the treatment towards its own workers.

Sincerely,
Rink Smittenberg,
Cambridge

34

We've faced the worst of the weather's blast, We've the guts, the strength, and the friends to last.

--from *Penrhyn Road Picket* by John Warner

LEAFLETING IN WINTER

Leafleting and picketing on a cold, snowy night, probably in 2005. The guards in the two pictures are Bob McLaughlin, Bill Kenney, Marilyn Leung, Carlos Oviedo and Jim Kowalski.

It is January, or is it February? I can't remember which. It is six degrees and we are leafleting in downtown Boston, above the Commons by the Boston Athenaeum. There were five or six of us, plus McCarthy, which was unusual, and I wonder why he was with us that day. Maybe I'm dreaming, but I remember clearly trying to get my fingers working with some semblance of skill and dexterity so that I could properly hand out our leaflets. I never quite achieved that, and often a person had already walked by before I was able to put the leaflet in my fingers and appear to hand it to them in a natural movement that indicated, "This is something important that you should read." They were half way down the block before I had properly embellished my introduction and presentation. Hopefully one of the other leafleteers would catch them. And, hopefully, they would read it. Having read it, hopefully they would be outraged. And being outraged, they would hopefully e-mail or call the Museum on our behalf and tell Malcolm Rogers what they thought.

"Well, here comes the next person. I'll try it with my gloves on. Nope! That's even worse!" I can't even begin to grasp a sheet of paper. "Oh, well, try again."

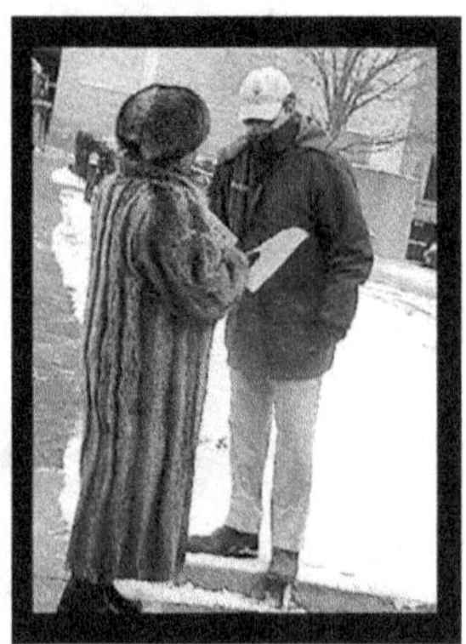

Mary Berry leafleting on a cold and snowy Martin Luther King Day in her fur coat.

My memory conjures up numerous variations on this theme:

Leafleting a Trustee Party at the Museum, the day after a two-foot snowstorm. Besides frozen fingers, there is snow up our knees. The snow is beautiful, but movement is close to impossible. The Trustees look at us as if we are crazy. But every so often, someone will take the sacred piece of paper and sometimes even read it. We persist. Even with the snow curling the pages and turning wet and mushy on the paper. We persist until the last partygoer has come and gone. Okay, good job, guys.

I remember we were standing by the T-stop on Huntington Avenue. Periodically, a train comes, and groups of varying sizes depart and head for the warmth of the Museum. It is ten degrees, so they go swiftly to escape the cold. I fan the leaflets so I can quickly hand out one after the other in quick succession. When successful, I am filled with a feeling of elation and triumph. If not, a feeling of dejection and clumsiness. But there is always the next train. I fan the leaflets and wait there. Another train approaches.

On another snowy night, Russell Gilfoy with his picket and leaflets. The leaflet is actually one which personalizes our message by giving a picture and little biography of one of the guards, in this case, Russell, himself.

Still again. Okay, eight degrees. There are just two of us giving out leaflets. Scott Faust, the Museum's lawyer, passes by chance. We exchange greetings and repartees. He even takes a leaflet and reads it. Why not? See what the enemy is up to. Faust is actually a liberal. I looked up his voting record. I wonder why he works for the corporate Museum. Could it be the money?

The contract campaigns begin during the time of year the last one left off. I often wondered if they tried to punish us by always ending the contract in winter.

35

All warfare is based on deception.

--Sun Tzu

ONE MAN IS A PICKET LINE

Joe McNeil was a sweet, kind inoffensive little old man who worked as a security guard at the MFA. Probably he was lonely. I never saw him with any friend and he smoked too much. His specialty was taking a visitor by the hand who had a question about where a certain painting or school of art was located and leading them directly to the desired area. He wasn't supposed to leave his assigned galleries, but somehow he, and he alone, was able to get away with it.

Anyway, it was our first contract campaign as an independent union and we needed someone to go out in the field and leaflet one of the Museum's corporate sponsors (I forget which one it was). Joe was our man.

Actually, we were a little nervous, wondering whether someone with a passive and non-aggressive personality like Joe was up for this job. When we tried to describe where the place was, we were dubious that he could even find it. But we gave him a small sheath of leaflets, crossed our fingers, and sent him off.

A few days later, we had a negotiation session scheduled. We were there early, got the best seats, and waited. After a while, the management team arrived. Scott Faust, their lawyer, was livid and shaking. In lieu of a gun, he pointed his quivering finger at us. "We will not negotiate with you as long as you have a picket line in front of our foremost corporate sponsor. You must absolutely promise to desist from this moment onward."

McCarthy was there, and he answered, "I'm sorry, but you cannot dictate what we will or won't do." "Well then!" said Faust, and he and his team stormed out.

When he was gone, we looked at each other. What the hell was he talking about? We had no picket lines. And then we remembered Joe. He must have leafleted a couple of "Suits". We imagined them stewing in the elevator. With each floor, the story must have grown. By the top floor Little Joe had become a bunch of big Joes. When the boss heard it, it probably grew still more. And when he called the Museum to complain, it grew yet more.

"It is not what you have, but what the enemy perceives you as having." Little Joe McNeil had become a fearsome picket line.

In the beginning Mary and Marilyn are a bit nervous as you can see. It's a little scary, especially for the ladies. I had to reassure them many times that there was nothing to worry about. In the background is an anxious employee of the corporate sponsor checking us out. She will surely report back to the bosses and the bosses will report back to the Museum.

I don't have any pictures of Joe, who has unfortunately passed away. But above are two pictures of Mary Berry and Marilyn Leung on a soiree in front of a Museum corporate sponsor in downtown Boston:

Here we are a little later at the same spot. You can see that Marilyn and Mary are much more confident and self-assured...and proudly happy at accomplishing their mission.

36

Noblesse Oblige, definition two: The obligation of honorable, generous and responsible behavior associated with high rank or birth.

--Merriam-Webster

CAN A MILLIONARE BECOME A GREAT HUMAN BEING?

Cornelius Vermeule III was a descendant of the Vanderbilts, but from the "poor side of the family," as he liked to say. Around the Museum, he was known as Doctor Vermeule. He had been head curator of the Classical Department since time immemorial, except for a stint as director of the Museum in the 1970s. He was respected as one of the best curators of his profession.

Like many of his colleagues of that era, Conelius had dealt with some gentlemen of dubious repute in order to get the finest treasures for the Boston Museum. The good doctor had a great sense of humor. Among the historical American coins in a certain glass case was a common copper penny "from the collection of Cornelius Vermeule III." He exemplified the better aspect of *noblesse oblige* and the "Museum Family." While he might not become a bosom buddy, he was genuinely concerned for all the employees of the Museum regardless whether they were administrator or cleaner.

Dr. Vermeule was kind of a hero to many of us guards. I am not exactly sure what Dr. Vermeule's status in the Museum was at the time of the Boston Massacre in 1999. He is listed as working from 1959 to 1997, but he was still physically very much around in the Classical Department in 1999 when the notorious purge took place.

Cornelius as we knew him.

While he escaped the purge of the Boston Massacre, he responded far differently than most of the other curators, some of whom stabbed each other in the back to get better jobs that suddenly became open, or hid away to escape collateral damage. Dr. Vermeule, in contrast, set up a kind of employment first aid station, where he used his extensive connections to help those who lost their jobs, or those whose jobs were in danger, to find employment in places with a more compatible and stimulating environment.

He also openly backed the union, even writing a series of articles for us in our newsletter. And I have to admit that I was personally indebted to him. One birthday of mine, he stated that the president of a union deserved a proper car to drive, worthy of his position, and he presented me with a brand new Rolls Royce. Of course, I must add that it was three inches long, but a gorgeous little model, cast metal with beautiful details. I held it in the palm of my hand in wonder and gratitude. I loved that model, only wishing I could take it for a spin around the block.

For his heroic stature and bravery, the Museum made him a *curator emeritus* (the same designation as Fairbanks got) and kicked him out the back door.

The following is one of a series of articles Cornelius wrote for our newsletter, *The Security Blanket:*

[Miss Daisie--Daisie (Fernandez) was, of course, a security guard.]

SECURITAS
by Cornelius Vermeule

She was a major personification in ancient Rome, "the well-being of the people of the state". Security used to be the name of our Department of Protective Services. Roman Securitas reminds us that what the activities of our colleagues who walk the Museum's galleries are all about are simply, people.

Consider that our "temple of the muses" is in the capable hands of our protective colleagues twenty-four hours a day, seven days a week. Administrators, Curators, and Facilitators come and go, but on open evenings, weekends, and indeed, all night, it is our Guardian Angels who interact with visitors and protect works of art priceless in value.

Over my fifty years of association with the museum, our Security Protectors (guards is too military a term!) have been many and wonderful people. To have discussed the game of cricket with Felix Martin is just one tiny measure of how much we all miss a truly wonderful human being. And for a number of summers Marian Stokes manned the check room in its so-called slow season. As a former teacher she shared her insights into the remarkable series of novels, historical and romantic that she read. When a young student writing papers on works of Greek art in the Museum, it was proverbial that Mr. Gonski (his classic dignitas precluded use of his first name) knew more about the Snake Goddess than did any college professors. He even used to write the papers for struggling students. There was the time Fred Bacon caught (like a fly ball) one of the marble heads inadvertently knocked off its pedestal in the Roman Court.

In a word, our colleagues on the "front lines" at the Museum are one of our greatest resources. I salute all my many friends among you, with love and respect. As Russell Gilfoy might say when we are speaking Greek together, "Na pate sto kallo", or "go forward with the best". And speaking of the best among you, I look forward to a chauffeur's career on retirement, driving Miss Daisie!

THE SECURITY BLANKET

Contributors:
Michael Raysson, Lisa Rhea, Dr. Cornelius Vermeule, Sergio Perez, Bruce McWhirk, Robert Nason

37

The man who has millions will want everything he can lay his hands on and then raise his voice against the poor devil who wants ten cents more a day.

--Samuel Gompers

THE UNLEVEL PLAYING FIELD

If I think back on my union days at the Museum, I can't get away from the fact that I was always looking uphill and management was always looking downhill. It was just the way the Game was played.

For instance, there is past practice. Say, technically, you're supposed to be at roll call 15 minutes early. But there is no reason for that except to wait around doing nothing. In fact, no one has ever done that, and management knew that and never called anyone on it. Suddenly, the boss starts disciplining people without any warning for being late to that 15 minutes early arrival time. That's where Robert Schwartz's book on winning past practice grievances comes in. With his help, or his book's help, we can probably, with a half-way decent steward, have the disciplines erased. But chances are, we won't be able to stop this sudden change in policy, even if it isn't necessary.

Robert Schwartz, the labor lawyer's labor lawyer, who wrote the bible on most union labor topics and who made the playing field a lot less uneven for us.

There is a big management's rights clause in every contract (some with more power, some with less). But, in most places of business, it allows them to pretty well run the place in the way they want. It does say that it has to be "fair and reasonable," but there is a huge legal leeway in determining what is fair and what is reasonable. Also, they are supposed to discuss changes with the union before they implement them. I used to think that was a big deal, like a negotiation, but it isn't. They don't really have to listen to anything we say unless they want to, which is very rare, indeed. If their mind is set on something, there is probably no way we can change it...But we *can* be a big pain in their ass, big enough so that they have to think if it is serious enough for them to go through the hoops we put before them in order to get what they want.

We can grieve the disciplines. We can grieve the fact that they unilaterally imposed new working conditions (without discussing them in GOOD FAITH). We can ask for loads of information that they generally have to supply. We can take the case to the National Labor relations Board. This will scare them the first two or three times, until they see how ineffective the NLRB really is. Their definition of good faith, it must be said, was most often our definition of bad faith.

Truly, those last two are just stalling tactics. But it can really be a pain in the ass for the boss. If you are consistently on their case, they just might learn that it is easier to discuss it with you in good faith with some chance for input by the union.

I took these discussions very seriously. I studied their point of view very carefully. I always came in (at least in my own eyes) with excellent alternatives that were more conducive to our needs. (It so happened, that once or twice, they actually used my suggestions.) Perhaps they might see that we were not just being troublesome, but that we could work with them if they let us. More likely, that is way too dangerous an expectation.

I have explained in a rational, legal way the unlevel (and totally frustrating) playing field. It is the way that management wants us to play. In the end, however, this is war. McCarthy well advised us never to depend on the legal system, if at all possible. It was indeed frustrating to put up with all that *bullshit*. In retrospect, however, I realize our *bullshit* was more frustrating for them than theirs for us. When I would walk past Malcolm, just seeing me, he would often express this frustration. So we had actually succeeded in getting under their skin.

Usually corporate management sees "working with them" as doing what they want. There will be a down to earth discussion between the two sides, and following that, everything is executed exactly as they wish it. What the union gets out of that kind of "working together" is the immense pleasure of being in the same room with the bosses.

So in the end it's not working the legal system that gave us a win. It was that they were never going to get anything from us without a fight, even if we lost. Somewhere in their consciousness, there was the idea that they might sometimes be better off just letting things go. Management should always feel in the back of their mind they will have to deal with "full court pressure." It is also called, *The People United Can Never Be Defeated*. And on top of that we could shame and embarrass them worse than they could bear.

The steward's job is such a tedious chore. Without them we would be out the door,
Fired for another yet unjust cause.
We cannot thank them all enough,
Because the job is so very tough.
--from *Stewards* by David G. Hurlburt

THE GRIEVANCE PROCEDURE

When UPGWA appeared to collude with Museum management (see the chapter titled *Betrayal)* and left the Union high and dry and the members demoralized, we fought and won against the Museum in an election for an independent union. Still, the guards were divided, and because of that, management got a clause in the contract where the guards employed at the time of the contract could choose whether to join the union or not.

At this point, we were saved, in large part, by the Grievance Process. That is, the first thing I did was to build a crack crew of shop stewards, who worked hard as hell to take the back of any guard who got into trouble with management. We learned which cases were winnable and which weren't. We learned how to investigate cases, what were the important points to look for, and how to find loopholes in management's case. We learned about Past Practice and establishing precedent. We learned why winning what seemed to be "bad" cases later helped to win "good" cases. We learned that if you let certain cases pass uncontested, that set an unfortunate precedent for all future cases of that nature—and vice versa.

I worked as a steward through much of my career and I found it to be a very interesting and rewarding job. Of course, I loved to overcome management's arguments and (evil) intentions. Originally, the vote for UPGWA was over 80% in favor. In the vote for an independent union we won by only seven votes.

Management learned that we were serious and our members learned that we were serious. And right there, the Union was made for the future. I cannot overstate how important that was. So important, that almost every one of our old members chose of their own free will to join the Union. Also, I overstate the value of having a consultant like McCarthy and a lawyer like Schwartz.

In the beginning, we used Schwartz a lot and were educated by him (quickly, too, because every time we called him, the meter was running). Later, we got to know the laws pretty well, as well as the modus operandi and the limits to which we could push things. We also learned how to deal with whoever was the director of Security (or Protective Services). John Paul Kozicki, who was only director for a short while (thankfully), was the exception. We just couldn't find a way of working with him. Most of the others realized that it would be valuable for them to work with us rather than constantly run into problems.

Management is often the Enemy, but if you make them an Implacable Enemy, incapable of being dealt with, you are lost. Make them feel good when they come round. Make them regret it when they don't.

We usually had around five stewards, sometimes even more, because we had full-time day crews and full-time night watch guard crews, and we had the part-time crews on weekends and nights, plus large overtime crews. We tried to have a steward around at all times. This was doubly great, because it enabled a large amount of guards to get the experience of working as a steward at one time or another.

We had steward training, of course, and I guess it worked well, because all the time I was there we won a good percentage of cases (quite often against the unfair legal odds we have mentioned). We set good precedents which would probably hold up in arbitration, although you could never be totally sure about the arbitrators, and we established the grievance system and the steward as the backbone of the Union.

Generally, the grievance system is management's domain. The laws are on their side. There are four steps in the process, and management adjudicates three of them, each time higher up on the chain. The fourth is Arbitration, and that alone is judged by a supposedly unbiased arbitrator. If, as a union you understand and work the system, both legally and strategically, so that you win your fair share of the cases, you are way ahead of the game.

39

People start to heal the moment they feel heard.
--Cheryl Richardson

LISTENING & HAVING FUN

Everyone wants to be listened to, whether they have ideas, problems, or just want to talk. They could be Kenny Peters, who could and would "talk your arm off," or Bill Kenny, who had cultivated the most extensive collection of trash talk known. It could be Mary Jane McCarty, who sometimes drove her co- workers crazy. Or it could be Allen Harrison, who was always pissing off Dave Skirkey (and could never understand why), or it could be Dave Skirkey, who was always pissed off at Allen Harrison. It could be Peggy, who always had one health problem or another. It could be Ron Gilbaugh, an inveterate, creative and likeable liar. Or it could be one of the hard-working Latina women.

I had two good teachers on listening skills. One was McCarthy. The other was my wife. My wife, of course, was the best.

Some few guards had my home phone number, and so I would hear of their scrapes at all hours. (A smart person would not let this happen.)

It was absolutely necessary to listen to as many people as possible before setting the goals and issues for a contract campaign. Not only did I have to know the important issues—but the order of importance. Because there comes a time when you have to drop some and stick with others to the bitter end. Even then it was necessary to listen to my fellow negotiators to see where their energy level and stamina were and where their fighting spirit was. Sometimes, you could pump that up, but sometimes it was obvious that it was either time to "cut bait" or come up with a stratagem to stall for time. Listening or not listening could be the difference between winning and losing.

Equally important was absolutely listening and listening closely when members had disputes with each other or grievances with management. In the case of member disputes, I found that only rarely was it possible to know who was really right or wrong—or how much right and how much wrong. I would listen to one side and it would seem as if there was no doubt that they were in the right. Then I would listen to the other side and magically it would seem as if there was no doubt that they were in the right. Mostly, I saw that I was never going to know the reality of the situation. And guess what, it somehow didn't matter.

If I really listened with full attention and with sympathy to each side, and made sure they knew that (you can't fake it), that was what really mattered. Often, the situation was righted as long as both sides felt their grievance or slight or whatever it was, was listened to and attended to as best as could be done.

If possible, I listened to management or at least the ones who cared to have a dialogue. For instance, Jim Beneway was head of security for a relatively long time. Many people hated him. But he had once been a guard himself. I always listened carefully and sympathetically to Jim. He had a good side and that good side cared. I appealed to that good side and often it worked. In the case of problematic issues or troubles between Jim and some guard or guards, I could usually make deals with Jim helpful to the guards. Of course, if he had orders to the contrary from above, forget it.

HAVING FUN

Once, I was up in the administrative office with the deputy director of the museum, the head of human resources and the Director of Security. I don't even remember why I was there. I do remember telling them that things were easy for them because they made big salaries, whereas, I had to worry about guards who could barely get by from week to week, and that was very difficult for me. The head of human resources looked at me and said, "You look like you're having a good time to us."

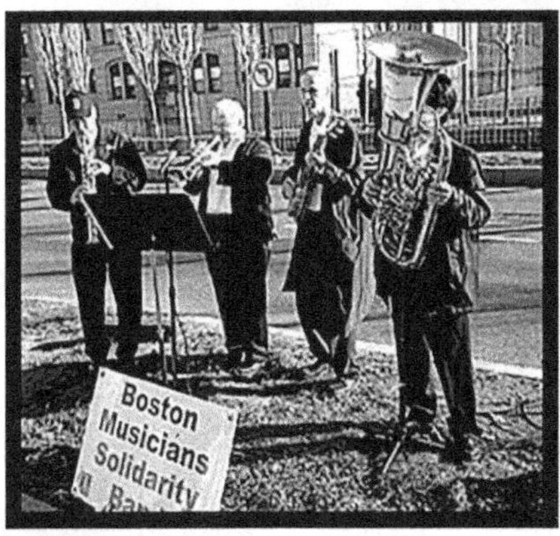

Norman Daoust (third from left) and his Boston Musicians Solidarity Band from the Musician' s Union made any demonstration more fun.

McCarthy also said to me, "You shouldn't be doing this work if it's no fun for you. If you don't like doing it."

Sometimes, I thought he was crazy when he said that. It wasn't always clear to me, because the job seemed onerous and the odds often seemed insurmountable. You know what? I realized that I *liked* insurmountable odds. I loved beating the corporate bullies. Somehow. Some way. So much the better if it seemed impossible.

Have I mentioned that McCarthy would often say, "Management is easy. It's your own people that are difficult."

Guards could have a good time dressing up in costume appropriate to the demonstration. In this case, the puppet character has a "security hat" on its head, and comes from a play we put on at a demonstration, called, Punch and Security (see appendix). *The puppet head was made by Sarah Peattie, a wonderful and magical lady who is head of the Boston Puppeteer Collective.*

The scrapes that guards got into with each other were even worse than the scrapes with management. I would go to bed with no solution in sight. Next day or next week, all would be O.K. At these times, a sense of the magical, the mysterious and the divine seemed to work.

I could complain that, with the exception of McCarthy and Schwartz, we had no professionals on our side. On the other hand, we accomplished everything on the grassroots level with just each other, our comrades-in-arms. Nobody, except those two, was paid to help us. Nobody was paid to catch us if we fell. It was walking on the tightrope backwards while juggling with no net. It was exhilarating.

40

There's folks standing tall who once lived in fear
There's folks standing tall who once lived in fear...
I've been many hard miles but one thing I'll swear
The union is a light in the face of despair

--from *Hard Miles* by Phil Cohen

OUR PEOPLE

Thinking back on it from the beginning when we met as a secret cabal, to my final moments sixteen years later, the cast of characters that was in the forefront of union activities at any particular time was ever changing. Not only that, someone who was my close friend at one moment could become an enemy at another. And the reverse was also true: many a fierce enemy changed into a close and faithful comrade.

Partly, of course, this scenario of a changing cast with changing loyalties came about because of the strange nature of the security guard work routine. Partly, it was because what might have been to someone's advantage at one point may not have seemed so advantageous at another. Finally, there was the heavy load of work that many carried, depending on overtime or second or third jobs, while others, such as students, were around only for a short stay before moving on.

But that was only part of the story. And stories there were, with deep plot lines and twists, some going on over long years, some, just a few days. I learned to never give up on anyone.

A watch guard worked totally different hours than a gallery guard, and a break guard, different hours still. Part time guard schedules were all over the place. Then there were people who worked mostly at the doors or in the coatrooms. Add on overtime or second and third jobs, as mentioned above. How hard it was to get them all together at one time. How hard it was to communicate. But we did.

There were black and white confrontations. There were locker room enmities that could last for years. Overtime fights and jealousies were brutal. There were fights over posts, and break guards were either the cause of, or the offended parties in huge hassles over timeliness. Somehow things worked out.

Once a union officer complained to a faithful union member about their body odor. The faithful union member never came to a union event ever again. And that feud still existed for decades. Just recently I found out that many years after I left, this member has, at last, forgiven the officer and is once again participating in Union demonstrations.

Jim Kowalski had the most difficult family life imaginable, working full-time and taking care of a needy brother with mental problems, also fulltime. In addition, his sister was a single mother, and Jim was instrumental in helping to raise her child. Still, he was at practically every demonstration we ever had. He was on most of our negotiating teams. He also was our first treasurer. He did it for a number of years, before it drove him crazy. It is my experience that treasurer is the hardest position to fill. Apparently, no one wants to deal with

Jim Kowalsk

all those figures and then be responsible for everything fiscal coming out all right. It is certainly one of the most difficult and nerve-wracking posts.

The Old-timers

There were three or four people who could be depended on year after year. These were special people who could be counted on to do the nitty gritty work behind the scenes, which made them practically indispensable. Russell Gilfoy, Jim Kowalski and John Storrow were stalwarts who were there at the beginning, who stayed there throughout.

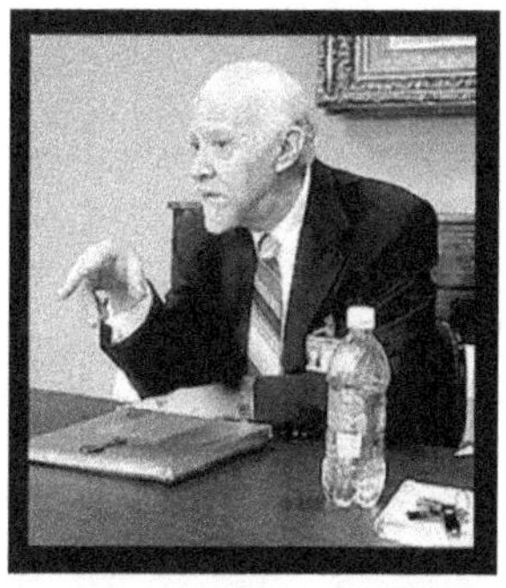

Russell Gilfoy making an important point at a caucus during negotiations

Russell Gilfoy: In his earlier days, Russell had been an art teacher in the Millis, Massachusetts school system, and he had helped to organize a Teachers' Union there. Due to health problems, he left that work and became a security guard at the Museum. It is hard to remember a Union event without Russell. Except for the very first negotiations with UPGWA, Russell was on all of our negotiating teams.

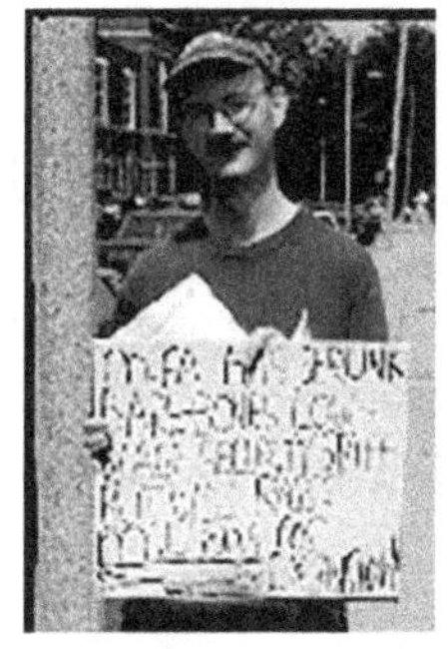

John Storrow, with his homemade sign

John Storrow: John was your plain old really good artist. Low key and in his own world, he was still kind of ever present. He put out our newsletter at times when it was crucial to communicate to members. He served as secretary and at negotiations. His wife, Lisa, was a guard for a while, and usually came with him.

John Moore was another guy who showed up. Also an artist, he was quirky as hell. He was also our last treasurer, and worked at it for many years. He was not easy to deal with because he kept a very tight hand on those purse strings. Later, after I left, he became a most ardent socialist. But that is another story.

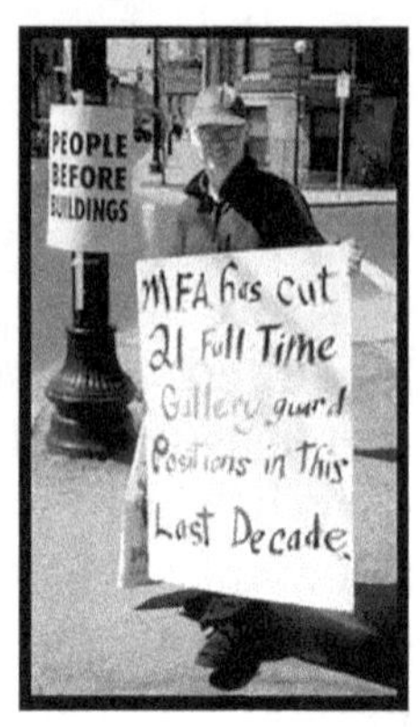

John and his home-made picket sign

Lisa Rhea (far right) with the author (center) and our local representative, Gloria Fox

Lisa Rhea: Like a volcano, at times passive and inactive, at times fiery as can be, Lisa had an unusual mind. At her best, I could strategize with her and bounce ideas back and forth. I could find out all sorts of intelligence, which she gathered from various sources because she had made friends with people in key positions. It was a pleasure to have someone like that with whom I could work, and at those times, I had a courageous comrade who was there to take my back.

However, this was only when the volcano was active. At other times, Lisa would slip into the background or become very self- protective.

I can remember negotiating sessions where Lisa threatened to whip the butt of some macho males, if they didn't step back in line. They knew she would have done it, too.

Lisa had been there right at the beginning in our first negotiations with UPGWA, along with Jill Abatemarco, Dave Hebden and myself. A couple of times, she, herself, assumed the president's position. At her best, Lisa was the most colorful comrade of them all.

Lisa's half-sister *Brenda Lee* had been at the Museum longer than anybody (and she's still there). She usually worked at the door. The docent ladies, the education ladies and the trustees whom she greeted there all loved her. Usually she sat back, but from time to time she used her position of eminence to whip the others in line, and whip she did. I remember when we needed to get all our members out for the big *Koch Rally*. Lisa said to me, with a wink in her eye, "Don't you worry, Raysson, they'll be out there."

Brenda Lee, our elder statesperson handing out leaflets.

Maureen Roe and Michael Scola also need to be mentioned as old timers who showed up regularly, sunshine, rain or snow. Maureen was a very sweet, shy and ascetic woman with a wry sense of humor. Mike worked as a union officer for a time, but the thing I remember him most for (aside from his reasonable counsel) was the time when we leafleted the Museum trustees. Trustee president Alan Strassman, a very unpopular (with us)

Maureen Roe

corporate CEO with a rather fierce persona, was leaving in his snazzy sports car. As he was about to exit the parking lot, Mike leaned over the window practically pressing our leaflet onto Strassman's face. Strassman, meanwhile, totally nonplussed, tried to act, unconvincingly, as if Mike and the leaflet weren't even there.

Michael Scola

Mary Berry: Mary was a really good person and a solid union worker. She became more and more involved toward the end of my career, especially during the last negotiation campaign. I had sort of hoped she could learn the ropes and take over when I left. But her husband firmly put an end to that idea.

Mary Berry at a caucus during negotiations

Union regulars from the various immigrant cultures of the MFA guard force

There was a large Latina contingent in the guard force (and also some Latinos). Every campaign saw a number of them participating as Union regulars. Most of them had families, but they still came out, always with enthusiasm and energy. Many were from Colombia, where a communal disposition seems to be the norm.

(Left above) Ovelis and Kendra,
leafleting on a snowy night
(Right above) Kendra (at left) with her daughter and Rosa Myers

Carlos Oviedo with Rose Lewis (right)
and an unidentified friend (center)

Carlos Oviedo. Carlos showed up midway during my career at the Museum. He was of a philosophical bent and brought with him the enthusiasm I have seen in quite a few Latin American organizers. I believe I have mentioned elsewhere how he could be depended on to arrive early at each and every demonstration with a bunch of signs stashed in his car. He also served as steward.

Robert Goldberg had been an eminent geologist

There also was a little enclave of Russian Jewish immigrants in the Museum guard force. Many of them had held important jobs or high achievements in the Soviet Union.

Eduard had been the number one ranked junior chess player in Russia. Nikolai was the elder statesman of the Russians. He was already at the Museum when I arrived and he worked there into his eighties. In a deep Russian accent, he would point at a young child and say, "Dangerous animal." He also would joke about taking his friends, fresh from Russia, to the Super Market, calling it a trip to the "Food Museum."

Marilyn Leung was a Chinese American who joined us towards the end of my career at the Museum. She was a very unusual woman with a lot of energy, serving as an officer, demonstrator and negotiator for us. She came with me to meet many of the politicians who helped us and took part in leafleting the corporate sponsors. She was also a movie actress, and I believe she had a part in a local Matt Damon movie towards the end of my stay.

Marilyn Leung (right) at negotiations with Mary Berry and Russell Gilfoy

Peggy Jarrett was a family woman from the Caribbean Islands. She had serious health issues at the time, both with herself and with her children, so it was hard for her to participate in anything but taking care of her family.

Peggy Jarrett (far left) at an MISU Union meeting. (Also pictured on her right are Tina, Elliott and Steve Buckman, sitting and Don Cusack, standing.)

Later, after I left and the museum was threatening to farm the guards out to a rent-a-cop company, I came back to help. Who did I see leading the troops out in front of the museum with a megaphone, but a now healthy Peggy.

Unusual (and extremely helpful) union members who worked at the Museum during differing periods

Gary Lombard was a wild card. Every union should have one. I have described how he single handedly kept our leafleting campaign going one year. Another time, he plastered the windows of Shreve, Crump, and Low, a faithful sponsor of museum exhibits, with our leaflets. They never sponsored another exhibit again.

Robert Nason was an excellent artist and a real gentleman in his eighties. For a while he ran the newsletter. As long as he was working as a guard, he was there on the front lines. His slogans and artwork almost always hit the mark. (See the Chapter, *Smart and Dumb Ideas*.)

There was one guy, *Scott Stevens*, who was just around for a year or so. I used to go on sorties with Scott to leaflet in front of corporations that were museum sponsors. For that year, he was my right hand man. He also often wrote articles in the newsletter. After the campaign, he disappeared.

Josh Lyons was a godsend, a type you get maybe one time only and consider yourself lucky at that. I guess I have already raved about him, but I will happily do it again. In addition to what I have already said, Josh meticulously researched our opponents. He found out everything about Malcolm Rogers and the MFA it was possible to find out, and then filed it precisely so we could use it in forming our strategy, when needed.

Joe Hodnick was another person who was just around for a short time, but who was incredibly important in those moments. In his case, that happened to be the transition from UPGWA to MISU. In the transition period, before the final vote on an independent union, we had to collect union dues by hand, person to person (as opposed to dues being automatically deducted from the pay check). If you think this is simple, let me say our experience was that "*pulling teeth*" is easier and less painful. At that time, there were also racially tinged disputes in the bargaining unit, and Joe was instrumental in handling them in a healthy, rational manner, with help from Anthony Meikle, a member who briefly and unexpectedly stepped forward in a leadership role.

Guard musicians

Among the membership were a number of musicians, some with large followings in the local area, but who hadn't caught on beyond that, and who needed an extra job. Most of these made their way to our union demonstrations where their (generally) jolly dispositions were well appreciated.

Gary McManus was one of the musicians, and he was a locker room favorite because of his large repertoire of jokes. Later he became a union officer and negotiator, and for a short while after I left was interim president.

Gary McManus at a Union meeting, between Tom Lynam and Rose Lewis.

Bruno Faria was a classical composer, and I remember he even got a commission from the government of his native Portugal. He also became president after I left.

Bruno Faria (left)

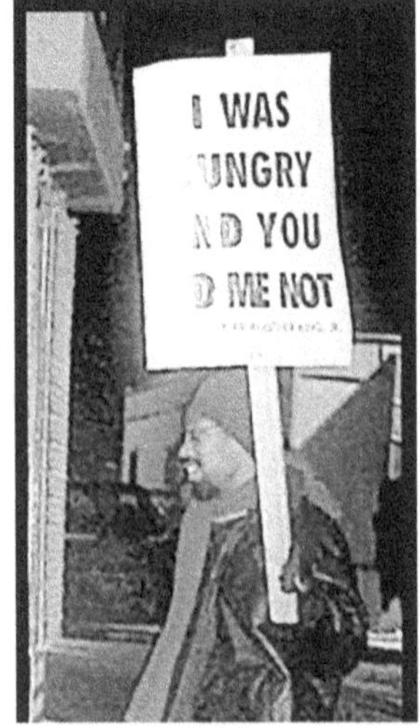

Another musician, *Stephen Holness*, a family man, was a shop steward. His wife worked nights and he worked days in order to get by, in addition to his music.

Valuable union members who proved you should never give up on anyone

After I persuaded *Don Cusack* to become a union member, he was well nigh indispensible. Don was one of our best members. He had been a school guidance counselor in his earlier days, and he was a good counselor for us. He was our *Eminence Grise and one of our best* resources for wisdom. After a while, he became a valued Union official and worked on some of our negotiating teams.

Bill Kenney, taking a class at the Boston Labor Guild

Bill Kenney, as I have said, had the most extensive repertoire of trash talk known to man or woman. He was habitual, and that got him in trouble with customers, and, as a result, with management. He was a pain in the ass. But he had some excellent ideas, which we sometimes put into action. He worked as a Union steward for a while, and he was a good one. He also became our man to keep an ever-vigilant eye on management to make sure the overtime process was being worked correctly (overtime being one of the biggest and most explosive issues among members that we had). For low-wage workers, who live from one week to the next, overtime can be the difference between getting by that week, or not.

And while I am remembering how important it is to never give up on anyone, *Mary Jane McCarty* immediately comes to mind. She always used to get into scrapes, especially with her fellow workers. To be true, she was over qualified. But I always listened to MJ as we called her, and if she had a viable grievance, I took it up. MJ appreciated that. At first, she used to hate me and hate the Union. But when she realized she could depend on us, and we had her back, she became a faithful union member who showed up regularly and contributed.

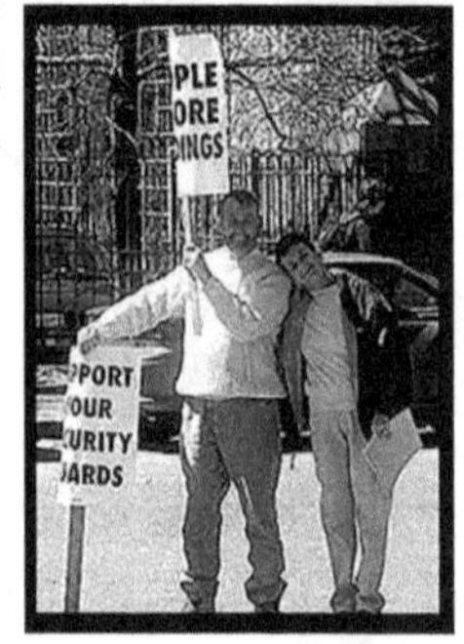

(Right top) MJ out there on a cold and snowy night. (Right bottom) Mary Jane and Bob McLaughlin

Non-union helpers, individuals and groups

Over the years, we got a lot of help from outside people. As a whole, union outreach to such kindred spirits and groups and to the outside community is indispensable. I am extremely grateful to many of these and I would like to talk about a few.

One guy whom I want to mention but was not a member of our bargaining unit was *Rich Giordano*, an aide for State Senator, Diane Wilkerson. I got to know Rich during our 2005-6 campaign, when we were working with all of our local politicians. I rarely saw Diane, but Rich was really there for us when we came to Diane's office, and was always extremely helpful. But what especially impressed me was that he went out of his way to attend many of our demonstrations, which he came to by bicycle, leafleting and picketing alongside the members.

Rich Giordano (Right)

Sarah Peattie in her magic studio/warehouse

I met *Sarah Peattie* when I came back to help the guards in 2012. She headed the Boston Puppeteer Collective. She gave a lot of time to help us and contributed any of her puppets that we wanted to use in our demonstrations. She asked for nothing at all in return but the joy of working with us.

Jobs With Justice is a great progressive organization with branches all over the country. I first met them when I was trying to find an alternative to UPGWA. That was way back when Rand Wilson was running the show. Then Russ Davis took over for a long while. Jennifer Doe was a lovely person and also a very important figure in JWJ while I was at the Museum. She came to some of our demonstrations and was immediately a charismatic presence.

JWJ put me in touch with all sorts of other groups and individuals and unions. They encouraged us to come out in solidarity when others needed help and encouraged others, in turn, to help us.

The Labor Guild is the closest thing to a continuously running labor union school. Once a week in the evening, after work, in fall and spring, they have eight-week courses in a wide range of subjects, such as "The Stewards Job", "Negotiating" and "Labor Union History." The teachers are all labor union people with extensive experience, who teach for free.

The *Carpenters' Union* was great to us. They were the ones who made up twenty- and thirty-foot banners for me. And they did it for free. Now and again, some of their members came to our demonstrations.

Those who died with their boots on

Finally, I need to mention a *bunch* of guards who *died with their boots on,* that is, while still working as security guards.

John Semedo was an elderly African American guard who had worked long years before I came and, afterwards, continued to work five or ten years more. At last, he was able to retire. Alas, just a couple of days later, he died. John had told me how in the early days, before the Union, the Museum management had stuck him to work in the basement, day in and day out.

Vinny Agri was another guard who was there way before I arrived. He lived by himself. One day, my friend Ed

Gonski, a guard who sometimes visited Vinny, found him dead in his bathtub.

Ellsworth Scott, known as Scotty, was another old-timer at the Museum who was important in our history. For a short time, he was president of the Union. His voice and opinion carried quite a bit of weight. In his eighties, still working at the Museum, he passed away.

Marilyn Wright was also at the Museum forever. In the end, she hobbled around on a cane, still doing her duty.

Alan Harrison was a night watch guard who followed Tibetan Buddhist teachings and also that of Eastern Orthodox Christianity. He was a good Union man and he would often regale me with tales of interesting religious personages he had met. He died while still working not long before I retired.

From left, Carlos Oviedo, Shirley Monroe, the author, and John Moore

Yes, this is the author at the time clock, just about to punch out on his last day at work.

And this is my going away party with some of my compatriots in the staff lounge at the Museum.

A recent trip to the Museum reminds me of the diversity and comraderie that we had (and have). With hugs and sweet words, I meet up with old stalwarts who are still working at the Museum. I meet Monique from Haiti and Anna from Columbia at the coatroom. We talk about old times. I see Nadja from Morocco and Marya, also from Columbia, in the galleries, with more hugs and reminiscences. I run into Tony, the photographer and Matthew, the artist, and we discuss the exhibits and how their work is going. At the front, Malcolm the portraitist tells me about the Security Guard exhibit in the front lounge. And Brenda, our eminence grieze, about whom I have already said much, after hugs for my wife and myself, brings us up to date about what is happening.

I have been working on this book, chronicling that time for several years. I am almost seventy-seven years old, and the perspective of age and remembrance has given new and increased meaning to the adventures that we shared in those stormy days building the union and fighting for our labor rights. I hope that this chronicle will help you, the reader, as you go to battle with your co-workers and neighbors and demand your rights.

APPENDIX

A TALK GIVEN BY STATE REPRESENTATIVE BYRON RUSHING AT THE SECURITY GUARD RALLY IN FRONT OF THE MFA, MAY 15, 2005

There is absolutely no reason why an institution with the budget of the Museum of Fine Arts should be attempting to get you to take less in any kind of contract negotiations. What is necessary here is that the Museum puts a moratorium on hiring any more part-time workers for guards. We should have a majority of the guards being full-time, if they wish to do so, so that they can get full-time benefits.

What is happening here at the Museum, of course, is straight out of management's guidebook to labor around the country, and that is to get rid of full-time jobs. Over and over again, it is to try to figure out ways of paying workers less. This is an important demonstration for all workers. What you are doing here is an important work for not only yourselves, but for workers throughout this city, throughout this state, throughout this country.

As Chuck pointed out, it you lived at the MFA and registered to vote at the MFA, you could vote for Chuck and you could vote for me and Diane and Gloria Fox. So we feel comfortable saying to the MFA, saying to Malcolm Rogers that what they are doing is unfair. What they should be doing is not attempting to be union busting, not attempting to discourage the organized workers in the Museum, and not trying to turn the workforce in the Museum into a totally part-time workforce.

Now, if the curators of this Museum knew what was

good for them, they'd be out here, too. A lot of workers in this building who aren't organized should be out here. They are being duped. They are being duped. You are telling not only the truth for yourselves, but you're telling the truth for all the workers in this building. You can bet if they can get away with this, that they will be working to get all the positions, the educational director, the curators, the antique curator, the near eastern arts curator, they will all be working to get them one of two things: consultant or part- time worker. That is the direction that this institution is going. And it is going in that direction probably because it has too many board members who work for companies or run companies that are doing the same thing. And they, as a non-profit organization with their budget, cannot use that as an excuse. It is not an excuse.

The MFA is probably, if you wanted to add up the cultural institution in this city, is the institution with the worst reputation and with the best publicity. No doubt about it. They probably pay more on publicity than they do on your combined salaries. With that publicity, they are able to get people in this city to think that somehow paying the admission to this museum is a bargain.

They are able to say that they do stuff for the community that surrounds them, when they refuse to do any fund-raising so that we can have a decent Museum of African Art in Roxbury. The Museum of the National Center of the African American Artist would not cost this MFA as much as they are spending on one new gallery, to fix up the whole building.

This MFA is a world-class disgrace when it comes to major art museums. The community surrounding the MFA is in the same relationship to this Museum that

Harlem was to the Metropolitan at the end of the 1960s. We are in that kind of situation. And what you are doing is just part of what all community people should be doing. And that is telling the truth about what is really going on at the MFA.

And finally I want to say, whatever we can do, we will do. I don't know if we are going to get an answer to this letter. If we don't get an answer to this letter, we will have to respond to Malcolm the same way we had to respond to the President of Northeastern. We will take it to his office. We will take it to his office. We will be there.

And finally, let me just say one of the silliest P.R. pieces that the MFA does, of course, is to tell people that they are working to try to involve more people in the Roxbury community and to have more people in the Roxbury community use the Museum. Well, the first thing they could do to do that is to tell the truth about their address. The MFA, Museum of Fine Arts of Boston is in Roxbury.

ACKNOWLEDGEMENTS

The author wishes to thank Muriel, who did everything, everywhere, in every way; Bill Gamson, whose inspiration in the beginning got me "to put pen to paper"; my good friend and neighbor, Michael Koran, who supported me all along the way, including editing, discussing, and having a continuous back and forth on this for the last couple of years; Dave Hebden, who was with me at the beginning of all this at the Museum, and, who, still around, helped me to kick around a lot of ideas; Paul, who, as usual, gave me words of wisdom and advice, some of which I took; Steve, who, when things were at their lowest, connected me up with Hardball Press; my friends and colleagues who read the manuscript at various stages, giving comments and suggestions, and who encouraged me to push ahead and get the thing published; Tim, from whom I have learned a whole lot of things I never knew and who has been a pleasure to work with; and, finally, all the security guards at the Boston Museum of Fine Arts.

TITLES FROM HARD BALL PRESS

A Great Vision: A Militant Family's Journey Through the Twentieth Century, Richard March

Caring: 1199 Nursing Home Workers Tell Their Story, Tim Sheard, ed.

Fight For Your Long Day, Classroom Edition, by Alex Kudera

Good Trouble: A Shoeleather History of Nonviolent Direct Action, Steve Thornton

I Just Got Elected, Now What? A New Union Officer's Handbook, 3rd Edtion, Bill Barry

I Still Can't Fly: Confessions of a Lifelong Troublemaker, Kevin John Carroll

In Hiding – A Thriller, Timothy Sheard

Justice Is Our Love In Action: Poetry & Art for the Resistance, Steward Acuff (author), Mitch Klein (Artist)

Legacy Costs: The Story of a Factory Town, Richard Hudelson

Love Dies – A Thriller, Timothy Sheard

The Man Who Fell From the Sky – Bill Fletcher, Jr.

Murder of a Post Office Manager – A Legal Thriller, Paul Felton

My Open Heart: 1199 Nursing Home Workers Tell Their Story

New York Hustle: Pool Rooms, School Rooms and Street Corner, A Memoir, Stan Maron

The Secrets of the Snow –Poetry, Hiva Panahi

Sixteen Tons – A Novel, Kevin Corley

Throw Out the Water – Sequel to Sixteen Tons, Kevin Corley

The Union Member's Complete Guide, 2nd Edition, Updated & Revised, Michael Mauer

Welcome to the Union (pamphlet), Michael Mauer

What Did You Learn at Work Today? The Forbidden Lessons of Labor Education, Helena Worthen

Winning Richmond: How a Progressive Alliance Won City Hall – Gayle McLaughlin

With Our Loving Hands: 1199 Nursing Home Workers Tell Their Story, Timothy Sheard, ed.

Woman Missing – A Mill Town Mystery, Linda Nordquist

The Lenny Moss Mysteries (in order of release) – Timothy Sheard

This Won't Hurt A Bit

Some Cuts Never Heal

A Race Against Death

Slim To None

No Place To Be Sick

A Bitter Pill

Someone Has To Die

One Foot in the Grave

All Bleeding Stops Eventually (2020 release)

Hard ball Press Children's Books on next page

Children's & Young Adult Books

The Cabbage That Came Back, Stephen Pearl (author), Sara Pearl (translator), Rafael Pearl (Illustrator)
Freedom Soldiers, a YA novel, Katherine Williams
Good Guy Jake, Mark Torres (Author), Yana Muraskho (Illustrator), Madelin Arroyo (Transslator)
Hats Off For Gabbie!, Marivir Montebon (author), Yana Murashko (Illustrator), Laura Flores (Translotor)
Jimmy's Carwash Adventure, Victor Narro (author), Yana Murashko (Illulstrator), Madelin Arroyo (Translator)
Joelito's Big Decision, Ann Berlak (Author), Daniel Camacho (Illustrator), Jose Antonio Galloso (Translator)
*Manny & the Mango Tre*e, Ali Bustamante (Author), Monica Lunot-Kuker (Illustrator), Mauricio Niebla (Translator)
Margarito's Forest, Andy Carter (author), Allison Havens (illustrator) Omar Majeia (translator)
Polar Bear Pete's Ice Is Melting! (A 2020 release) Timothy Sheard (author), Kayla Fils-Aime (Illustrator), Madelin Arroyo (Translator)
Trailer Park, JC Dillard (Author), Anna Usacheva (Illustrator), Madelin Arroyo (Translator)

www.ingramcontent.com/pod-product-compliance
Lightning Source LLC
Chambersburg PA
CBHW030242030426
42336CB00009B/213
9781734493825